MARCO ◉ POLO

Travel with **Insider Tips**

AUSTRALIA

INDON.
East Timor
Timor
Darwin ○

Coral
Sea

AUSTRALIA

○ Brisbane

Perth ○

Canberra ○ ○ Sydney

Melbourne ○

Tasman
Sea

INDIAN

OCEAN

Tasmania

D0774023

SYMBOLS

INSIDER TIP	Insider Tip
★	Highlight
● ● ● ●	Best of ...
☼	Scenic view
☺	Responsible travel: fair trade principles and the environment respected

PRICE CATEGORIES HOTELS

Expensive	over A$140
Moderate	A$90–140
Budget	under A$90

The prices are for a double room without breakfast

PRICE CATEGORIES RESTAURANTS

Expensive	over A$25
Moderate	A$15–25
Budget	under A$15

The prices are for a main dish without drinks

On the cover: Diving with rays, manatees and whale sharks p. 100 | Above the roofs of Sydney p. 37

CONTENTS

Queensland → p. 68

Northern Territory → p. 84

Western Australia → p. 96

Road atlas → p. 154

DID YOU KNOW?

MAPS IN THE GUIDEBOOK

(156 A1) Page numbers and coordinates refer to the road atlas
(0) Site/address located off the map. Coordinates are also given for places that are not marked on the road atlas
(U A1) refers to the street map of Sydney inside the back cover, Melbourne → p. 61, and Perth → p. 107

**INSIDE BACK COVER:
PULL-OUT MAP →**

PULL-OUT MAP 🗺

(🗺 A–B 2–3) Refers to the removable pull-out map
(🗺 a–b 2–3) Refers to additional inset maps on the pull-out map

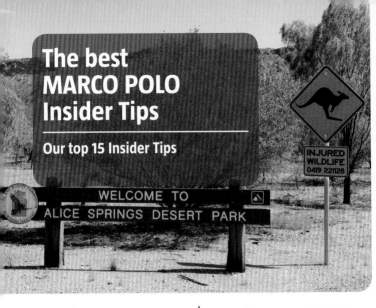

The best MARCO POLO Insider Tips

Our top 15 Insider Tips

INSIDER TIP **A trip around paradise**

Cape Range National Park has a variety of natural geological features, fossils and hundreds of flowering plants and is best explored with *Ningaloo Safari Tours* → **p. 100**

INSIDER TIP **Saddle up and gallop away**

Something special for horse-lovers are the hacks organised by *Reynella Rides* through rivers and the eucalyptus forests of the Snowy Mountains → **p. 138**

INSIDER TIP **Traditional way of life**

A Koori guide explains the everyday life and culture of the *Boon wurrung* and *Woi wurrung* Aborigine tribes in Melbourne's Botanic Garden → **p. 61**

INSIDER TIP **Kicking around Down Under**

Visit a 'footy' match – as Australian rules football or 'Aussie rules' is called with tens of thousands of wild fans in Melbourne → **p. 23**

INSIDER TIP **Pretty fishing township**

An inviting beach with lovely countryside further inland: *Apollo Bay* is *the* port of call when driving along the *Great Ocean Road* → **p. 65**

INSIDER TIP **Australian animals**

In *Wilsons Promontory National Park* on the peninsula of the same name on the south coast, you can see marsupials unique to Australia such as wombats, kangaroos and koalas and also watch emus, all sorts of water fowl, dolphins and seals → **p. 67**

INSIDER TIP **Remote gorge**

A visit to *Carnarvon National Park* is an unforgettable trek that takes you back to the time dinosaurs roamed the earth and to cultural sites of the Garinbal Aborigines → **p. 75**

INSIDER TIP **The tropical north**

Cape York is for those who want to experience raw nature and Aboriginal culture from close quarters → **p. 80**

BEST OF ...

GREAT PLACES FOR FREE
Discover new places and save money

● *Art for art's sake*
Contemporary art fans can enjoy themselves without paying a cent in the *Museum of Contemporary Art* on Sydney's waterfront. The exhibitions include works by international artists as well as an important collection of top-quality Aboriginal art → p. 35

● *Funky Friday*
Gypsy, jazz, Latin, folk, swing: Rektango, one of the best-known bands in Tasmania, has been playing for free on the Centre Courtyard in Hobart every Friday for more than 10 years → p. 126

● *Patient patients*
In the *Koala Hospital*, a large animal clinic run by volunteers in Port Macquarie, koalas are nursed back to good health and returned to the wild. The best time to visit is 3pm when the cuddly marsupials are fed → p. 54

● *Free transport*
No tickets are needed for the *City Circle tram* that travels right round Melbourne's city centre. Many sights can easily be reached on foot from the tram stops (photo) → p. 62

● *Fun in the city*
As the tropical town of Cairns doesn't have a decent sandy beach, a generously sized recreational oasis has simply been created between the pedestrian precinct and the coastal promenade with saltwater pools, a sun-bathing area and BBQs. The *Esplanade Swimming Lagoon* is a popular meeting place – and its free → p. 79

● *Adelaide Greeters*
That's what these friendly folk who greet visitors and show you around the city call themselves. The free service is provided by volunteers and is available every day between 9am–5pm → p. 118

●●●● Dots in guidebook refer to 'Best of ...' tips

● *Undersea marvels*
Visitors to *Sydney Aquarium* can see more than 650 creatures that live in the waters around about without getting their feet wet. An artificially laid out coral reef gives an idea of the beauty of the Great Barrier Reef (photo) → p. 33

● *Shopping with style*
The elegant *Queen Victoria Building* in Sydney has survived since colonial days. Go for a shop and take a step back to the days of the first pioneers → p. 38

● *Hands-on politics*
In *Parliament House* in Canberra you can see for yourself how Australia is governed. Regular guided tours provide a fascinating look behind the scenes in the day-to-day running of the country → p. 53

● *Immigrants and their history*
How did the first immigrants to arrive on the continent survive the arduous trip across the sea, cooped up with no room to move in small stalls under deck on wooden ships? The exhibition in the *Immigration Museum* in the former Custom's House in Melbourne provides plausible answers → p. 60

● *Creature comforts*
Lone Pine Koala Sanctuary is the largest koala animal park in the world as well as being home to other native animals. On the outskirts of Brisbane you can come face to face with platypuses, gawky flightless birds, tame kangaroos and cuddly marsupials → p. 73

● *Just give it a taste*
Do as the locals do (well, almost). The innovative food served in the popular *Ochre Restaurant* in Cairns incorporates Aborigine bush foods: emu, kangaroo or crocodile meat, local berries and bush tomatoes → p. 79

● *Sleep on the wild side*
The unusual *Gagudju Crocodile Holiday Inn* building – that looks like a croc resting in the sun – nestles in the unique natural landscape of the Kakadu National Park → p. 94

BEST OF ...

welcome

● **How things came about**
The extensive collections in the *Australian Museum* in Sydney provide a fascinating insight into the changing geological history of the ancient continent → p. 34

● **Doing time**
Avoid the rain – behind bars! Thick walls, bare cells, gloomy passageways and the old gallows in the *Old Melbourne Gaol* testify to the harsh sentences once passed in the former British colony of Victoria → p. 60

● **Shop till you drop**
Some 180 shops and countless restaurants and snack bars fill the multi-storeyed *Melbourne Central* shopping centre. You can easily spend hours here (window-) shopping in this air-conditioned consumer palace → p. 64

● **Underground tour**
It doesn't matter what the weather is doing when you're underground. Guided tours through the galleries in the *Hard Times Mine* in the remote mining town Mount Isa are a pleasant respite from the heat or rain in the outback → p. 72

● **Rock in the rain**
An unusual natural wonder is not to be missed at *Uluru (Ayers Rock)* when it pours with rain. Torrents flow down the smooth sides of the monolith, waterfalls plunge from far above and fountains shoot out of openings in the rock → p. 88

● **Mona – Museum of Old and New Art**
This ambitious private museum outside Hobart is an art experience of a special kind: visitors can touch objects, nose around, watch experimental videos till the cows come home and wander among works from Antiquity to the present day → p. 124

RAIN

● Sydney Tower
Relax more than 200m (656ft) above the city while enjoying a panoramic view in all directions – extending as far as the Blue Mountains on a clear day. When night falls, the lights in the city below sparkle away. The *Tower Restaurant* is a delight for all the senses – not just the taste buds → **p. 37**

● Relaxation in the park
The *Royal Botanic Gardens* are Melbourne's green lung. An extensive, well looked-after park along the quiet banks of the Yarra River with foot and cycle paths, shady avenues of trees, flower beds and neatly trimmed lawns – just perfect for relaxing → **p. 61**

● Luxury island hopping
A holiday on *Hayman Island* is not cheap. But this elegant resort off the coast of Queensland pampers its guests in a way one would expect from a luxury destination. This can include a visit to the *Hayman Spa* with its *Ocean Massage* → **p. 72**

● A refreshing dip
The freshwater lake fed by the *Edith Falls* in *Nitmiluk National Park* is a refreshing place to relax under the tropical sun well out of the way of crocodiles. Just dive in, wash the hot dust from your skin and gaze out at the rocky wilderness beyond the shore → **p. 95**

● Super sandy beach
22km (14mi) long: *Cable Beach* near Broome is just right for a snooze on the sand and a refreshing swim in the Indian Ocean. And as you chill out in the evening, you can enjoy the usually spectacular sunset → **p. 97**

● Tasty and inviting
Both bon-vivants and those seeking peace and quiet can find what they want in pretty *Barossa Valley*. This rural area spoils its guests with cosy places to stay, choice wines and hearty food → **p. 115**

INTRODUCTION

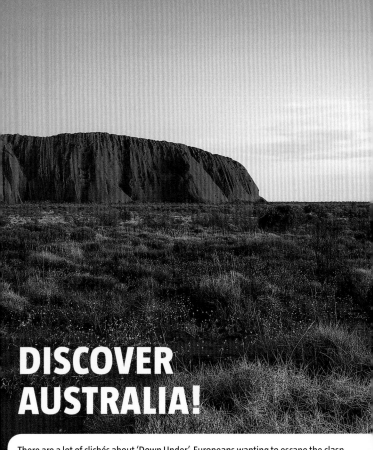

DISCOVER AUSTRALIA!

There are a lot of clichés about 'Down Under'. Europeans wanting to escape the clasp of modern-day civilisation may well dream of sitting around a campfire with Crocodile Dundee in person just after landing – or at least of meeting his brother. But the reality is a little bit different. Australia is a country with one of the highest rates of urbanisation in the world – with the majority of the 23 million 'Aussies' living in cities and towns.

Office workers with their ties flapping, who scurry through the urban canyons of Sydney or Melbourne in the morning and meet up with others in a pub in the evening for a quick refreshing Toohey's or a Victorian Bitter, are just as much part of this as the hordes of youngsters who seek out the vibrant night life at weekends, culture vultures who never miss a theatre performance, sailors, surfers and water rats who hang out on the yolky-yellow sandy beaches such as Bondi Beach in Sydney or Scarborough Beach in Perth, or the gays and lesbians in their wild costumes at the huge Sydney Mardi Gras Parade.

Photo: Uluru (Ayers Rock)

Brisbane has developed in the last few decades into an international metropolis

> **Multi-cultural diversity is the name of the game in this country**

Diversity is the name of the game in this country – and if you want to see people from 140 different countries living closely side by side then you should head for Melbourne. The generally problem-free multi-culturalism in Victoria's capital is the result of several major influxes of immigrants, such as those in the 1950s. But the Australian touch is always to be found – the 'no worries, mate' sounds just as genuine from the mouth of a Greek in Sydney, a German in Adelaide or a Turk in Melbourne as in Darwin or Alice Springs.

70,000–64,000BC
Aborigines arrive in Australia along a stretch of land from what is today Indonesia

1770
Captain James Cook maps the east coast and claims the continent for the British Crown

1788
750 convicts and their guards land in what is today Sydney. The British Crown used Australia as a penal colony

1851
Gold is discovered in Australia. The Gold Rush attracts people from all over the world

One continent – one state: this huge land mass between the Pacific and the Indian Ocean covers 2,966,000mi², an area almost 32 times the size of the UK. Caught between the extremes of western civilisation and the exotic outback, Australia is a unique cultural experience and an unforgettable adventure: magical coral marine parks and the Great Barrier Reef in the east and dusty bushland in the west, vibrant metropolises along the coasts and uninhabited deserts in the country's interior, the dense green of the tropical rainforests in the northeast and barren geological formations such as Uluru (Ayers Rock) in the red heart of the country, lush meadows in New South Wales and parched earth in Western Australia.

The Australian touch is that casual, laid-back joie de vivre you can really only find Down Under. Where else in the world does a nation grind to a halt for one whole day just because of a horse race – when the thrills and spills of the Melbourne Cup flicker across the television screens in every living room? Where else other than in Adelaide can you find a nationally important food festival where young and old, workers and managers sip top-quality wine, nibble choice tit-bits and chat away happily with one another? You can sample the delicious ingredients that make up the light Pacific cuisine grown in 'God's Garden' – as many farmers call the fertile south and southeast region – for yourself, in all their glory, in the gourmet restaurants in the towns.

They're flexible, the townies. When out and about in the bush far away from urban centres, even self-styled Sydneysiders, snobby Melbournians and lounge lizards

1901
The British colonies vote to become federal states within the Commonwealth of Australia

1915
The Gallipoli campaign in the Ottoman Empire (now Turkey) results in the death of thousands of Australian soldiers who were keen to support their mother nation, Great Britain, in World War I

1942
Japanese bombers attack the north Australian city of Darwin

1967
90% of Australians vote for equality for Aborigines

from Adelaide can turn into real bush-men types, happy to exchange disco beats for country music from the radio or perhaps a sing-along to 'Waltzing Matilda'. Then they put on their long socks and shorts, roll up their sleeves and don a sweaty Akubra, strap boats to their 4×4s and get out their fishing tackle. And, much to the surprise of many a tourist, the party clown from Adelaide or the Rotary Club member from Melbourne can put up a tent just as quickly and properly as they can drive an all-terrain vehicle safely across huge sand dunes.

They always return happy from such excursions and usually go into ecstasies about the wonders and beauty of their country. For many people from other corners of the globe who are more used to a critically sombre tone in their dealings with others, this may well be one of the nicest experiences of all – the daily lesson in positive thinking, the daily dose of good mood, the beaming nature of the Australians. 'No worries, Mate.'

Australia is a mixture of unexplored tropical or moderately cool rainforests and craggy, sometimes snow-covered mountain peaks with, of course, a good portion of adventure. Some routes for 4×4s, such as the Canning Stock right across Western Australia, still pose a danger even for the wiliest of adventurers. And when bush trekking in Wooronooran National Park around Mount Bartle Frere in Queensland, you really can get so hopelessly lost in the rainforest that a rescue party has to be sent out. On such trips you don't need to waste time asking for permission to camp or fish and there are no fault-finding foresters to stop you lighting a fire. When you sit there gazing at the starry firmament in the outback that – thanks to the dry air and the virtually complete darkness – sparkles as if it had just been given a good polish; when you can feel the earth cooling down from the heat of the day; then you'll find yourself plum in the middle of an Australia familiar from slide shows. However, some of the threats and dangers, such as crocodiles or some of the most poisonous snakes in the world – without which it wouldn't be an adventure – actually turn out to be less dramatic than you thought. Not few Australians see their country not as a continent but rather as an island that Mother Nature made a generous size, on which a number of appealing peculiarities and oddities from the early

1988
Australia celebrates 200 years since the arrival of the first Europeans.
Aborigine groups protest against 200 years of European occupation

2000
Summer Olympic Games in Sydney

2007
Australia suffers from years of drought; water reserves in some towns run dry.
Kevin Rudd (Australia Labor Party) replaces John Howard after eleven years as Prime Minister

2010
Kevin Rudd resigns, Julia Gillard becomes Prime Minister

days of the settlers have survived, such as a love of cricket and tea – a legacy of the British to the Australians.

'The Lucky Country' does, however, have its problems of course. The culture of the Aborigines, one of the oldest in the world, may well fascinate tourists, the brightly-coloured dot paintings of many Aborigine artists may well decorate living room walls, and boomerangs, hand-made by the native inhabitants, may spin through the air,

The Daintree National Park is a Unesco World Heritage Site

but behind this façade the social fabric is showing signs of wear. In 2004, there were massive racial riots in Sydney for the first time. Aborigines still have a hard time finding a job and an even harder time finding somewhere to live, as the opinion of the native inhabitants held by the better-situated Australian is more or less shared by everyone, and the billion-dollar social measures devised to assist Aborigines created more envy than new jobs.

There is no doubt that Australia, as a young nation, is still on the road to self discovery. Since the Summer Olympic Games in 2000 in Sydney, the lovely national anthem 'Advance Australia Fair' is played just that

Australia is a young nation

little bit louder – a heart-felt declaration of love to the nation and its pioneering spirit: 'We've golden soil and wealth for toil; Our home is girt by sea …" The text was originally written back in the days of the first settlers and gained its status as the official anthem in 1984, replacing the British national anthem 'God Save the Queen'.

WHAT'S HOT

1 Eye-catchers

Nightlife highlights Australia's nightlife is really exceptionally good. Every venue has its own style: in up-market *Ruby Rabbit* you will (almost) feel like royalty *(231 Oxford Street, Sydney, photo)* whereas in *Cocoon Bar* things are a bit cosier *(195 Swanston Street, Melbourne)*. Quite the opposite is true in *The Croft Institute* with its barred windows and austere interior *(21 Croft Alley, Melbourne)*.

DIY surfboards

Wood and bamboo More and more surfers are making their own boards. There are even events organised now where like-minded people can meet up, such as on *Wooden Surfboard Day* on the Gold Coast *(Currumbin Alley)*. Among regulars is the company *Hollow Wooden Surfboards* that fortunately also sells its boards *(Mount Eliza)*. At *Tree2Sea*, workshops are held regularly where you can find out how to make an eco-board yourself *(www.treetosea. org)*. There is a guide to making your own board on the Internet site of the *Riley Surf Team* that tackles the waves on balsa wood boards *(www.balsasurfboardsriley. com.au; photo)*.

2

3 Disc meets basket

Disc golf The rules are easy: the frisbee simply has to land in the basket. And then it's off to the *Rob Hancock Memorial Disc Golf Course (Mulligan Drive, Greenwood)* in Perth or the *Maze Disc Golf Course (1635 Neaves Road, Bullsbrook)*. That's where the *Perth Disc Golf Club* fights it out *(www.perthdiscgolf.com)*. If you want to battle against Sydney's team head for the Olympic Park *(www.sydneydiscgolfclub.com)*. In Tasmania, the course is picturesquely located in the *Poimena Reserve* in Austins Ferry *(Wakehurst Road, photo)*.

Melbourne's docklands

Up and coming In next to no time Melbourne's port has been transformed from a neglected area into a trendy district. The promenade alone with its cafés, bars, art venues and architectural gems is 7km (4½mi) long – and the project still hasn't been finished yet. Explore the area at your own pace on a *public art walk*. Route descriptions can be found under *www.docklands.com*. A walk can easily be combined with a bit of shopping – the best selection of shops being in the huge *Harbour Town Mall (122 Studio Lane)* where time passes in a flash! After night falls the docklands are anything but dead. How about a round of mini golf in the dark with a view of the city skyline *(Black Light Mini Golf, Star Crescent)*? Or perhaps you would prefer to finish off the day in *Livebait (55 B Newquay Promenade, photo)*?

New-media art

Moving with the times John Tonkin is one of the leading new-media artists in Australia. He collects data online before depersonalising it and presenting it visually in projects such as 'Strange Weather'. Most of his works can be shown as installations but also work online *(www.johnt.org)*. *Stelarc* is a performance artist who draws on his own body for inspiration *(www.stelarc.org)*. His work and that of other contemporary artists can be seen in the *Scott Livesey Galleries* in Melbourne *(909 A High Street, Armadale)*. Another place to seek out is the *Art Gallery NSW* that awards a video and new-media prize – last won by David Haynes and Joyce Hinterding *(Art Gallery Road, Sydney, photo)*.

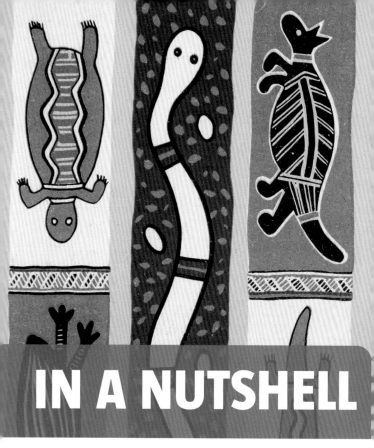

IN A NUTSHELL

ABORIGINES

According to the latest findings, Aborigines left the African continent some 64,000–75,000 years ago and arrived in Australia by way of Asia. This makes the Aborigine culture the oldest outside Africa. And it remained isolated until the first white men landed on the continent at the beginning of the 17th century. Although Aborigines enjoy the same rights today as Australians of other backgrounds, this equal status is something that exists primarily on paper. The medical care in many Aboriginal communities is catastrophic with experts putting it on a par with that of third world countries. The native inhab-itants of Australia die on average 7 years earlier than other Australians. Ignorance and undiluted racism shown is part of everyday life for many Aborigines. The gutter press generally paints a negative picture and is one of the reasons that many Australians see the indigenous minority as a kind of blot on their country. This atti-tude is in stark contrast to that of tourists, many of whom come to Australia explicitly to find out more about the oldest culture still in existence. It was only in 2008 that the Prime Minister at that time, Kevin Rudd, gave an official apology, in which he said 'sorry' three times for all the in-justice to which Aborigines have been

Photo: Aborigine works of art

Picnics, sport and real men: facts and interesting things to know about modern-day Australia

subjected and especially for the so-called 'stolen generation'. Up until 1970, children were taken away from their families and brought up in white households. See: *www. indigenoustourism.australia.com*

FILM INDUSTRY

The Australian film industry is a success story even if many film stars such as Nicole Kidman, Cate Blanchett, Russell Crowe or Mel Gibson came to fame in Hollywood rather that back home. Australian productions have also achieved international acclaim with box-office hits such as 'Muriel's Wedding', 'Crocodile Dundee', Babe or the epic drama 'Australia', starring Nicole Kidman and Hugh Jackman. Australians like going to the cinema and, as a nation, more cinema tickets are sold per capita than anywhere else. Films that focus on the austere life in the outback or on minority groups have achieved cult status, such as the comedy about three drag-queens in 'The Adventures of Priscilla', 'Queen of the Desert'.

FLORA AND FAUNA

Thanks to its isolation, Australia's primeval flora and fauna evolved undisturbed. After the demise of the dinosaur, mammals came to the fore in other parts of the world. In Australia, it was the mar-

and snakes are highly poisonous. The most bizarre of all creatures in Australia are the monotremes – that lay eggs and produce milk. Platypuses, that look rather like otters with ducks' beaks, and echidnas (spiny anteaters) are the only surviving representatives of this ancient order of mammals.

FLYING DOCTORS

The first medical emergency service by air in the world began in 1928 as the *Australian Aerial Medical Service* in the small town of Cloncurry in Queensland,

Platypuses live in rivers and lakes on mainland Australia and in Tasmania

supials. Kangaroos are just one of the almost 180 different species of marsupial. Many of the 40 sub-species of kangaroo in Australia are as small as rabbits; others grow to more than 6 feet tall and there are even some that can climb trees. Australia is a paradise for reptiles and insects. Most are harmless but some spiders

after the Presbyterian pastor John Flynn had seen the misery of those living in the outback for himself. Being so far from medical help, many people died as the result of injuries and illnesses that would have been treated easily in towns. Today, the *Royal Flying Doctor Service (RFDS)* operates from 21 bases.

HELPFULNESS

A particularly nice characteristic from the pioneering era has managed to survive to this day – the seemingly boundless helpfulness of the Australians, regardless of whether you have a puncture in the outback or have lost your way in Sydney or Melbourne. Appointments are rescheduled to be able to get you back on the road, maps are organised, routes explained – and all with a patience and friendliness that make most Europeans gasp in amazement. At such moments you really experience how strong the bond between Australians actually is and that the solidarity they feel for one another – at least among the white population – is one of the nation's fundamental values.

IMMIGRATION

Like Canada and the USA, Australia is also a coveted destination for immigrants. For more than 200 years, millions of immigrants have contributed to the country's identity. Today, one in four of the 23 million Australians comes originally from another country or has parents who were born abroad. Without them, there would be no modern Australia. Depending on the political climate and economic situation, Australia takes between 60,000 and 185,000 new arrivals from all around the globe every year.

MATESHIP

'Mateship' is a typically Australian phenomenon that bonds men like blood-brothers even today. In days gone by, only 'real men' had any chance of survival in the wilderness of this unexplored continent. Their common situation strengthened such bonds and helped make survival possible. On festive occassions today, the majority of Australian men still tend to stick together.

MUSIC

Australia's very lively music scene is more than just Kylie Minogue, that pop icon who still causes a furore internationally. Anyone who takes a closer look at life down under cannot avoid but coming face to face with rock giants like AC/DC and INXS, or Paul Kelly, Australia's answer to Bob Dylan. Unlike anyone before him, the songwriter from Adelaide has captured the Australian soul in his music since the 1980s. Local pop and rock bands, such as Powderfinger from Brisbane, often shoot to fame. Aborigine bands such as Yothu Yindi, with their frequently critical songs, also have large groups of fans.

NATURE & ENVIRONMENTAL PROTECTION

While the very first explorers in the 18th century had to battle with an overpowering and unknown natural environment, this situation has barely changed today. In the middle of the Kakadu National Park,

Airstrip for flying doctors

R.F.D.S. EMERGENCY

AIRSTRIP

bulldozers roar away quite casually in their search for uranium and gold; the Great Barrier Reef could only be rescued from being drilled to bits by oil companies by pulling out all the stops. And even the inundation of tourist hype contributes to the environment being damaged. *Greenies*, as environmental lobbyists in Australia are affectionately called, are often considered stark raving mad and labelled economy-killers – 'eco', for ecologically sound, is only really gladly seen on tourist brochures.

However, the wind of change has set in. Australia has even discovered climate protection for itself quite recently and is introducing a CO_2 emission tax, intended to deter air polluters, based on that in Europe. That something is not right with the climate can be felt in the increasing frequency of natural catastrophes. Vast areas under water after terrible storms in Queensland or devastating bush fires after continuous periods of drought in New South Wales and Victoria. The dry continent is in danger of dying of thirst or the earth becoming too salty – this is the warning of the horror scenario that is largely painted for the southeast of the continent where agriculture is only often possible thanks to artificial irrigation.

PARLIAMENTARY SYSTEM

The Australian parliamentary system is basically modelled on that of Great Britain and North America. But it does have its own features. The government comprises members of a parliament elected by the people and is divided into two chambers, the House of Representatives and the Senate. The government and parliament are located in Canberra. The party or coalition that has a majority in the House of Representatives forms the government. The Head of State, Queen Elizabeth II, appoints a Governor-General proposed by the government as her representative.

Australian rules football ('footy' or 'Aussie rules') attracts tens of thousands of fans

An alternative to the school canteen: picnicking is popular

PICNICKING

Australians are passionate about picnics. There are benches in the shade and tables, water and barbecues in almost every park and in rest areas along highways. Picnics are organised whenever a suitable possibility arises: by candlelight, with proper crockery spread out on a tablecloth before a concert or play, on the beach, on public holidays and before sport events.

SPORT

An enthusiasm for sport can be felt both actively and passively. Sometimes things can get a bit wild, for example during a so-called INSIDER TIP *footy* match when 36 players struggle to get their hands on an oval-shaped ball using all their bodily force. This is only topped by rugby, whereas cricket is bound to the traditional British reserve of fair play. Down under, football is only referred to as soccer and is enjoying increasing popularity since Australian teams recently gave a respectable performance at an international tournament. However, if the number of registered members in a sports club is anything to go by, the most popular sport in Australia is tennis.

TALL POPPIES

Australians react very sensitively to arrogance and presumptuousness. *Tall poppy syndrome* is what they call it when celebrities claim too much of the limelight – either through a nervous gaggle of bodyguards or, as in the case of politicians, through too great a distance to the man on the street. Tall poppies, many people think, have to be brought back down to earth again.

FOOD & DRINK

Australia is a paradise for lovers of fresh, light and varied food. Immigrants from all over the world have brought their eating habits with them. Thanks to the continent's various climatic zones, they have been able to grow their native vegetables, fruit and crops here too.

There is a stunning variety of fresh salads, exotic types of vegetable and tasty fruit available in the markets and countless little shops in Australian cities. And everything is grown in Australia – juicy fragrant mangos, sweet pineapples, bananas and coconuts from the tropical north, aromatic peaches, passionfruit, melons, litchis and citrus fruit from Victoria and New South Wales, apples and pears from Tasmania, choice grapes from South Australia – to mention just a few. On top of this there are numerous Asian leafy vegetables, tender broccolini, nutty avocados, sweet potatoes and not least of all a huge selection of fresh herbs and spices. Meat comes from cattle and sheep raised naturally on open pastureland – and from kangaroos, emus and crocodiles. The large fish markets stock everything the ocean, rivers and lakes have to offer, such as tender white barramundi from the saltwaters of the north, and John Dory from the bottom of the ocean, excellent fresh tuna, orangy-red

Photo: A café next to the Opera House in Sydney

The new Australian cuisine is a delightful mixture of light Mediterranean food with an Asian influence

salmon, delicious giant crabs, oysters and other shellfish.

Culinary wonders however are more on the rare side in the far-flung corners of the outback. Here, the food is often still 'traditionally Australian'. Immigrants who arrived in Australia in the 1950s and '60s look back in horror at some of the dishes that originally came from England – bland pies, leathery steaks and chops with mushy vegetables and 'salads' made with a few limp lettuce leaves and one tomato. The only alternative was the local 'Chinese-Australian' restaurant that dished up rice with tinned peas and carrots, and pork smothered in a bright-red, sickly-sweet sauce from the bottle. The best food came from the traditional barbecue – an evening of huge, charcoaled slabs of meat, charred onion rings, ketchup and white bread.

LOCAL SPECIALITIES

▶ **Barbecued prawns** – marinaded and grilled Australian prawns (photo above left)

▶ **Barramundi fillet with Macadamia nuts** – the delicious white meat of the barramundi served in a thin coating of chopped Macadamia nuts and a side salad

▶ **Kangaroo burger with beetroot** – low-fat kangaroo meat in a breadroll

▶ **Leg of lamb with roasted vegies** – cooked with garlic, rosemary and honey and served with roast potatoes, carrots, turnips and diced pumpkin

▶ **Meat pies** – small pies with an often undefinable meat filling and tomato sauce. A British legacy, traditionally served at football matches

▶ **Pavlova** – delicious freshly-picked berries, peaches, kiwis and the juicy middle of passion fruit on top of a meringue creation that is as light as a feather and fresh cream (photo above right)

▶ **Tasmanian salmon with bok choy and chilli jam** – fish and steamed Chinese cabbage in a fresh chilli sauce with ginger, brown sugar, vinegar and lime juice

▶ **Wattleseed damper** – bread baked in an earth oven with the nutty seeds of the wattle tree, served hot with butter and honey

▶ **Witchetty grub** – a maggot some 4 inches long and as thick as a finger that lives in the roots of the acacia tree. A food traditionally eaten by Aborigines in the desert either raw or cooked in embers. Tastes like a mixture of a nut and a hard-boiled egg

▶ **Yum cha** – a selection of Chinese specialities such as pastry rolls with crab and fresh herbs, dumplings with a cooked beef filling or steamed Chinese vegetables

Today, authentic food from all over the world can be enjoyed in many districts in Australian cities. Vietnamese soup kitchens rub shoulders with Italian pasta restaurants, classy French bistros are next to Indian take-aways, Greek tavernas opposite specialist Lebanese diners. And along with these, restaurants have emerged that focus on modern Australian cuisine – a delightful mixture of generally Mediterranean fare with a strong Asian influence. Several restaurants also use home-grown figs, bush tomatoes, sweet seeds and flowers from the outback that are part of the traditional diet of the Aborigines. Low-fat kangaroo meat that tastes like a cross between beef and venison, is prepared for gourmets and tourists in particular.

The average Australian housewife now offers her guests more than traditional roast lamb – tasty fresh stir fries from the wok, Thai soups with coconut milk, delicious moussaka or home-made pasta. Even the old Australian barbecue is often no longer what it used to be: meat is now marinaded in exotic sauces or cooked gently on skewers next to crab and fish, sizzling away in aluminium foil. All this is served with salads, dips and Italian or Turkish bread.

Chilled beer that lacks something of the taste and zest of European beers is drunk everywhere. This, however, does not apply to the sometimes excellent beer produced by the various small boutique breweries. Australian wines are excellent: earthy dry reds and refreshing whites – these are world class. German and Italian immigrants took the first proper vines with them to Australia and, today, Australian wine is exported around the globe. In some Australian restaurants with 'BYO' on the door, you can (or have to) bring your own bottle. Alcoholic drinks can often be bought next door in a 'bottleshop' that may well be connected to a pub. Restaurants open bottles and cool them for you – and charge a corkage fee *(approx. A$5–8 per bottle)*.

Coffee has evolved into an absolute delight in Australia, thanks to Italian immigrants who, from the early days, started importing their highly-polished espresso machines from home. In the meantime, the Aussies have developed a coffee culture of their very own. If you order a 'short black' you'll get a plain espresso; a 'long

The veranda of a café in Glenelg

black' is two-thirds water and one-third espresso. Extremely popular – and something of an invention from Australia/New Zealand is the 'flat white': one-third espresso topped up with two-thirds hot (but in no way frothy) milk, not to be confused with 'latte' (milk coffee) or cappuccino.

SHOPPING

Over the past 30 years, Australia has grown from being a shopper's nightmare into a shopper's paradise. At least in the larger towns you will find simply everything, and typically Australian souvenirs are sold even in the remotest of places in the outback. Only the 20–30 kg baggage allowance in the economy class of airlines could prevent that shop 'till you drop urge. But if it's all too much to resist, take advantage of the shipping service offered by many retail outlets – especially in the case of more cumbersome souvenirs. Those who do struggle along with their booty can at least reclaim the 10% VAT, provided that you have acquired the goods in a shop within 30 days of your departure, that they cost more than A$ 300 and that you can show both your purchase and the receipt at the TRS counter at customs when leaving.

ABORIGINAL ART

There are many mass-produced articles on offer that no Aborigine ever had anything to do with – whether bark paintings, wooden sculptures, boomerangs, clap sticks or didgeridoos. On the other hand, it is difficult for most people to determine what is a genuine crafted item or work of art and what is not. You can, however, rely on certified Aboriginal art galleries and Aboriginal cultural centres, e.g. at Uluru (Ayers Rock). And check the label of authenticity that has a registration number indicating which artist made the item.

CROCODILE LEATHER

Belts, bags, wallets or boots: products made from the leather of farmed animals are not a problem to import into Europe providing you have the relevant certificates. The export of kangaroo or possum pelts is also allowed. This is not the case for coral or shells of protected sea creatures – their export is prohibited.

OPENING TIMES

During the week, shops are generally open from 9am–7.30pm. In larger towns, late night shopping continues until 9pm. On Saturdays, smaller shops close at 5pm at the latest; on Sundays shopping arcades

Akubras, boomerangs and didgeridoos: typically Australian souvenirs can be bought almost everywhere

open their doors from 10am–4pm. A tip for market fans: a complete summary with a search function can be found under *www.marketsonline.com.au*.

OUTDOOR CLOTHING

Akubra is the name of the traditional Australian headgear. This wide-brimmed hat made of the best rabbit fur felt, that protects the wearer from the scorching sun as well as downpours and sandstorms, should really be bought at the start of you trip. They can be found in all sorts of shapes in hat shops or outdoor outfitters such as R.M. Williams. Quality Akubras – and only these can deal with the extremes of the Australian weather – come at a price. The same is true of Driza-Bones, as the waxed coats are called in which stockmen in the outback face up to the elements, or indeed of leather ankle

boots which really protect your feet over impassable terrain.

PRECIOUS STONES AND PEARLS

Near Broome in the north of Western Australia, elegant culture pearls are farmed in the coastal waters whereas valuable sapphires and opals are dug from the earth in the interior of the continent. The best prices are to be obtained locally, e.g. in Coober Pedy. The jewellery shops in the major cities work against this by offering unusual mounts. For the more bold, buy an unpolished stone or a pearl without a setting and have your gem fashioned by your local goldsmith at home. In the case of opals: the pale stones are the cheapest; those that shine in all colours of the rainbow are the most expensive.

THE PERFECT ROUTE

THE SOUTHWEST: COUNTRYSIDE AND COMFORT

1 *Perth* → p. 106 welcomes you with its urban charm but without the hustle and bustle of other major cities. The journey to the south passes idyllic beaches with a chance of seeing dolphins and whales out at sea. At **2** *Margaret River* → p. 103 you enter a land of plenty in which restaurants conjure up culinary highlights and where guests are spoilt with luxurious places to stay in the middle of wonderful country-side. To the north, **3** *Nambung National Park* → p. 109 baffles visitors with its weird desert landscape peppered with limestone pillars.

CITY FLAIR IN THE SOUTH

Fly to **4** *Melbourne* → p. 58 (photo left) and explore the most European city on this continent – with its impressive cultural life and fascinating countryside nearby. **5** *Phillip Island* → p. 66 with its wonderful beaches can be recommended, as can the **6** *Wilsons Promontory National Park* → p. 67 surrounded by the sea.

A REWARDING ISLAND HOP

Fly on to Tasmania and start a round trip in **7** *Hobart* → p. 124, passing **8** *Cradle Mountain/Lake St Claire National Park* → p. 120, and on to **9** *Port Arthur* → p. 126 (photo right) where you can find out more about the dramatic history of the penal colony in the days under British rule.

COAST TRIP

Back to Melbourne and off down the **10** *Great Ocean Road* → p. 133 with stunning vistas, and on to **11** *Adelaide* → p. 110. Perhaps you'll have some time to make a detour to the rock paintings in the **12** *Grampians* → p. 56 or to the paradisiacal nature reserve **13** *Kangaroo Island* → p. 117.

RIGHT THROUGH THE COUNTRY'S RED HEART

The legendary train journey on 'The Ghan' terminates in Darwin. En route you are surrounded by the outback as far as the eye can see – and have a welcome break in the desert town **14** *Alice Springs* → p. 84 – with the opportunity of taking a 5½-hour bus trip to **15** *Uluru (Ayers Rock)* → p. 88.

IN THE TROPICAL NORTH

16 *Darwin* → p. 89, the capital of Northern Territory, is the perfect starting point for an adventurous trip to the untamed wilderness of

Experience some of the facets of Australia on a round trip with detours to the Grampians and Uluru (Ayers Rock)

17 *Kakadu National Park* → p. 93 with its dangerous saltwater crocodiles and the massive termite hills in **18** *Litchfield National Park* → p. 93.

GREAT BARRIER REEF AND SYDNEY

The plane to Cairns brings you to Queensland's popular holiday coast and the fantastically coloured coral of the **19** *Great Barrier Reef* → p. 68. The dense tropical rainforest is also within easy reach. The onward journey southwards towards Brisbane can be interrupted at attractive island resorts on the Whitsundays or Fraser Island. If you're in a hurry to get to **20** *Sydney* → p. 32 – the hub of modern-day Australia and the largest city on the continent – book a place to stay in the centre from where you can reach many of the sights on foot, and hop on a plane.

17,000km (10,600mi). Travel time only: 10 days. Recommended time for this trip: 3–4 weeks. Detailed map of the route on the back cover, in the road atlas and the pull-out map

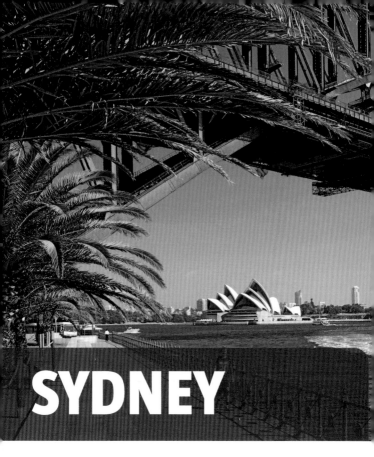

SYDNEY

MAP INSIDE BACK COVER
(177 E5–6) (*M J6*) **The white 'shell' roof of the Opera House glistens in the bright sun set off against the palm trees in the Botanic Gardens.**

Sailing boats and ferries cut across the blue waters of the harbour spanned by the steel arches of the Harbour Bridge. This is the heart of the city of Sydney with a population of 4½ million – a vibrant, multi-cultural metropolis and the capital of the oldest Australian state of New South Wales. Sydney covers a vast area, stretching more than 100km (62mi) down the coast and some 70km (44mi) inland. The bus network is well developed and

the most important sights can be reached on the hop-on hop-off buses *(www.city-sightseeing.com)*.

WHERE TO START?
Circular Quay (*M b–c2*) on *Sydney Cove*, where the railway station and bus terminal are, is the perfect starting point. Most sites can be reached on foot. Driving within the city is not recommended. Take a local *CityRail* train and get out in the city centre *(Wynyard, Townhall, Central)*.

Photo: The Sydney Harbour Bridge

Sea, skyscrapers and beaches: for many people, both locals and visitors, Sydney is the most beautiful harbour city in the world

SIGHTSEEING

AQUARIUM ● (U A4–5) (🚝 a4–5)

The long transparent tunnel takes you through an undersea world. The artificial Barrier Reef with its tropical fish and classical music is simply stunning. *Aquarium Pier | Darling Harbour | daily 9am–10pm | A$28 | www.sydneyaquarium.com.au | train: Town Hall | ferry: Aquarium Pier |* monorail: Darling Park | Sydney Explorer Bus: stop 24

ART GALLERY OF NEW SOUTH WALES ★ (0) (🚝 0)

The gallery boasts works by Australian and international artists and includes the Yiribana Gallery with the largest permanent collection of Aboriginal art anywhere in the world. *Art Gallery Road | The*

Domain | daily 10am–5pm | admission free, free guided tours 11am, noon, 1pm, 2pm through various galleries | www.artgallery. nsw.gov.au | bus 441 from York Street (Queen Victoria Building) | Sydney Explorer Bus: stop 6

INSIDER TIP ▶ AUSTRALIAN MUSEUM ●
(U C5) (𝄞 c5)

Carnivorous giant kangaroos, monster wombats and dinosaurs with razor-sharp teeth – Sydney's natural history museum provides a fascinating and often humorous look at the evolutionary history of the Australian continent and its people and animals. *6 College Street | daily 9.30am–5pm | A$13 | australianmuseum.net.au | CityRail to Town Hall, then on foot along Park Street*

AUSTRALIAN NATIONAL MARITIME MUSEUM (U A4) (𝄞 a4)
Located right on the water in a basin in Darling Harbour. The exhibits show the

Monorail in Darling Harbour

importance of the sea and seafaring to the inhabitants of the world's smallest continent. *2 Murray Street | daily 9.30am–5pm | admission free, Navy Ticket A$20 | www.anmm.gov.au | bus 443 from Circular Quay or York Street | ferry from Circular Quay to Pyrmont Bay | monorail to Harbourside Station*

CIRCULAR QUAY ★
(U B–C2) (𝄞 b–c2)

This is where all ferries come in – with easy connections to the trains and central bus station. The wide harbour promenade on Circular Quay goes from The Rocks to the Opera House. An unforgettable experience, providing a completely novel panorama of the city, can be had in a INSIDER TIP ▶ sea kayak on a quiet, guided paddling trip around the harbour, bookable through *Sydney Harbour Kayaks | tel. 02 99 60 43 89; Captain Cook Cruises organise harbour trips with lunch/dinner, daily 9.30am–8pm | from A$60 | No. 6 Jetty | Circular Quay | tel. 02 92 06 11 22 | www.captaincook.com.au*

DARLING HARBOUR/KING STREET WHARF (U A4) (𝄞 a4)
This former maritime industrial area is now an attractive development of shops and restaurants. Performances are regularly held here at weekends on various open-air stages. *Monorail, lightrail or with the Matilda Rocket Explorer from Circular Quay (every 45 mins. from 9.55am | www.matilda.com.au*

HARBOUR BRIDGE ★ (U B1) (𝄞 b1)
Some time ago Sydney Harbour Bridge, opened in 1932, could only be admired from afar. Since 1998 you can climb it too. The 3½-hour tour is now one of Sydney's most popular attractions and is often booked out days in advance. No cameras allowed. The highest point (134m/440ft)

is reached up steel ladders, across metal links and steps. *Bridge Climb | 5 Cumberland Street | The Rocks | from A$208 | tel. 02 82747777 | www.bridgeclimb.com | bus/CityRail/ferry to Circular Quay, then on foot through The Rocks*

INSIDER TIP ▶ JUSTICE & POLICE MUSEUM (U C2) (*m c2*)

In what was once the old harbour police station until 1890, a fascinating and sometimes spine-chilling insight into the deeds of gangsters and crooks in and around Sydney can now be enjoyed here today. The restored magistrates court, several remand cells and a collection of murder weapons, as well as artefacts of the legendary Ned Kelly Gang are among the highlights. *Albert/Phillip Street | Jan daily 10am–5pm, Feb–Dec Sat/Sun 10am–5pm | A$11 | on foot from Circular Quay*

MUSEUM OF CONTEMPORARY ART ● (U B2) (*m b2*)

Andy Warhol is here as well as Christo and other famous contemporary artists from

The Harbour Bridge was opened in 1932

around the world. Unusual gifts can be bought in the small museum shop and tasty food is served in the MCA café. *140 George Street | Circular Quay/The Rocks | daily 10am–5pm | admission free | on foot from Circular Quay*

MARCO POLO HIGHLIGHTS

OPERA HOUSE ★
(U C1) *(🗺 c1)*

The glistening shell-like roof of the Opera House, located right on the harbour, has become Sydney's landmark. The Danish architect Jørn Utzon won an architectural prize with his revolutionary design – and the right to build the Opera House in Sydney. After seven years of battling with Australian bureaucrats who said the project was too expensive, Utzon gave up. His work was only completed after a 14-year building period – and with help from the lottery that provided the necessary funding. The opera theatre, the concert hall and several smaller theatres are all housed in the building. *Sydney Opera House | Bennelong Point | guided tours daily 9am–5pm (A$35) | www.sydney operahouse.com | bus/CityRail/ferry to Circular Quay, then on foot along Circular Quay East | buses 324, 325 and 438*

THE ROCKS ★
(U B2) *(🗺 b2)*

The Rocks at the western end of Circular Quay is the oldest part of Sydney. In 1788, convicts erected the city's first proper buildings on solid rock foundations. The sandstone structures that now line the quay and the narrow cobbled streets date from the early to mid 19th century. In the 1970s the historical buildings were to be demolished to make way for skyscrapers. The Builder's Labourers Federation however refused to knock them down. In those days the police were sent in; today The Rocks is a conservation area. Due to its proximity to Circular Quay and the many pubs and restaurants, The Rocks *(www.therocks.com.au)* has long since developed into a popular tourist area – the open-air weekend market being a special favourite. The pretty *Rocks Discovery Museum (2–8 Kendall Lane via Argyle*

Jörn Utzon's most famous building: the Opera House

Street | daily 10am–5pm | admission free | www.rocksdiscoverymuseum.com) is a reminder of times gone by. The 90-min. INSIDER TIP Rocks Walking Tours *(Mon–Fri 12.30am, Sat/Sun 11.30 and 2pm | 23 Playfair Street | tel. 02 92 47 66 78 | www.rockswalkingtours.com.au) | bus/CityRail/ferry to Circular Quay* brings history back to life.

ROYAL BOTANIC GARDENS ★
(U C2–3) *(ፙ c2–3)*

The botanical gardens in Sydney are on the most beautiful of the bays on the harbour, not far from the Opera House. This was where the fields on the first farm in the penal colony were once established. The original section of the gardens, where Australian trees and plants in particular can be seen, was laid out in 1816.

A well-maintained path leads from the Opera House along the waterside to ◣ *Mrs. Macquarie's Chair*, a seat hewn out of the rock. From here, the wife of the erstwhile governor sat and watched the goings-on in Sydney Harbour. The cool grove of palm trees with countless flying foxes, the large herb garden and the glazed Tropical Centre are fascinating. *Daily 7am–8pm, March–Oct 6.30pm | www.rbgsyd.nsw.gov.au | CityRail to Circular Quay, Martin Place or St James*

SYDNEY TOWER EYE ◣ ●
(U B–C4) *(ፙ b–c4)*

The *Observation Deck* (approx. A$28) is one of the easy ways to see Sydney from above as is a visit to the *Tower Restaurant* or *Café (tel. 02 82 23 38 00 | Budget–Expensive)*. It gets a bit more adventurous if you take the 1½-hour *Skywalk (daily 9am–10pm | tel. 02 93 33 92 00 | www.skywalk.com.au | from A$68)*, as the 268m (880ft)-high platform has a glass floor! The 360° panorama is magnificent and an audioguide explains the sights. *Pitt*

In the Royal Botanic Gardens

Street/Market Street, Centrepoint Shopping Complex | www.sydneytowereye.com.au | monorail Centrepoint

TARONGA ZOO
(0) *(ፙ 0)*

Excellent collection of Australian animals. The nocturnal house, the daily Seal Show with rescued sea lions and the Free Flight Australian Bird show are particularly worth a visit. *Head Road Bradleys | daily 9am–5pm | A$44 | www.zoo.nsw.gov.au | ferry from Circular Quay (free in combination with a zoo ticket, information in the visitor centre)*

FOOD & DRINK

Many – and more particularly – good restaurants can be found around Circular Quay and in Darling Harbour *(Cockle Bay Wharf* and *Kings Street Wharf)*. Further away from the city centre, head for *Oxford Street* in Darlinghurst and *Bayswater Road* and *Macleay Street* in Kings Cross and Potts Point. If you fancy seafood, don't miss a visit to INSIDER TIP *Sydney Fish Market* for a delicious lunch of fresh prawns and oysters *(Pyrmont Bridge Road/Bank Street | light rail to Fish Market)*.

INSIDER TIP BAMBINI TRUST CAFÉ
(U C3) (*m c3*)
Exquisite food and atmosphere; the coffee is specially flown in from Italy. Tip: order a 'coffee/latte to go' during the day and head for Albert Park next door. *185 Elizabeth Street | closed Sat/Sun | CityRail to Martin Place*

IL BARETTO (0) (*m 0*)
Not expensive and yet very good – Sydneysiders love such places which means it is always packed at all times of day. Serves specialities from northern Italy as well as hearty pasta dishes and pizzas. *496 Bourke Street | tel. 02 93 61 61 63 | closed Sun | Budget–Moderate | bus 389 to Darlinghurst (Stanley Street)*

HARRY'S CAFÉ DE WHEELS
(0) (*m 0*)
True gourmets may not want to be spotted here. Harry's has been serving its famous pies for decades – with all sorts of Australian meat fillings and other variations. *Cowper Wharf Road | tel. 02 93 57 30 74 | open every day | Budget | bus 311 to Potts Point*

MANTA (0) (*m 0*)
The décor in this restaurant is unpretentious – black wooden tables, white walls and few pictures. The same goes for the food: wonderfully fresh oysters are served without any frills as is the Arab-style octopus. *The Wharf at Woolloomooloo | Cowper Wharf Road | tel. 02 93 32 38 22 | open every day | Expensive | bus 311 to Potts Point*

OPERA KITCHEN
(U C1) (*m c1*)
The prominent square outside the Opera House right next to the harbour bay is made for dining outside on a mild summer's evening or for a pint of beer before sunset. You can let your gaze sweep across the water, watch elegantly dressed opera goers and sample, for example, dishes inspired by Asian cuisine that are made from the best raw ingredients available. *Lower Concourse Level | Bennelong Point | www.operakitchen.com.au | daily from 7.30pm | Budget–Moderate | Circular Quay*

INSIDER TIP SAILORS THAI CANTEEN
(U B2) (*m b2*)
Loud and delicious. Everyone sits at one (long) table: very authentic Thai cooking. *106 George Street | The Rocks | closed Sun | Moderate | bus/CityRail/ferry to Circular Quay, then on foot along George Street*

WILDFIRE
(U B1–2) (*m b1–2*)
This, Sydney's gastronomic shooting star, has won all sorts of awards for its creative cuisine (citrus cured ocean trout). Reservation advisable. *Ground Level Overseas Passenger Terminal | Circular Quay West | tel. 02 82 73 12 22 | open every day | Expensive | to Circular Quay, then on foot along Circular Quay West*

SHOPPING

The grand sandstone buildings along *Strand Arcade (255 Pitt Street | CityRail to Town Hall)* (U B4) (*m b4*) and ● *Queen Victoria Building (455 George Street | CityRail to Town Hall)* (U B5) (*m b5*) house elegant boutiques, designer shops and tea shops.
Unconventional fashions can be found on *King Street (bus 422)* (U B4–5) (*m b4–5*) in Newtown and *Glebe Point Road (bus*

433) (0) (𝓜 0) in the student district Glebe. Several top Australian designers have boutiques on *Oxford Street* (U C6) (𝓜 c6) in Paddington *(bus 333 to Darlinghurst Road)*. This is also where by far the most popular market in the city is held every Sat around St John's Church *(www.paddingtonmarkets.com.au)*. Authentic Aborigine

Walk, a 3km (1¾mi)-long path along the coast, between the residential area Vaucluse to the east and Dover Heights, past the sandstone cliffs to Diamond Bay. Keen hikers head further south following the path to Bondi and still have enough stamina for the 6km (3¾mi) coastal walk to Coogee.

Shopping in wonderful surroundings: Queen Victoria Shopping Market

art is sold at *Hogarth Galleries Aboriginal Art | 7 Walker Lane | Paddington | www.aboriginalartcentres.com | bus 389 to MacDonald Avenue* (0) (𝓜 0) and *The Aboriginal & Tribal Art Centre | 117 George Street | walking distance from Circular Quay* (U B3) (𝓜 b3).

SPORTS & ACTIVITIES

You can easily leave the city behind you even on foot, e.g. on the *Federation Cliff*

BEACHES

Sydney's more than 30 beaches stretch almost 100km (62mi) down the coast. ★ *Bondi Beach*, the most famous and now on the National Heritage List, can be reached by regular buses or the Bondi Explorer Bus from Circular Quay. There is less going on at *Tamarama, Bronte* and *Clovelly Beach. Coogee Beach* is a pretty family-friendly beach with hotels, restaurants and cafés. Some beaches also have rock pools, perfect for relaxing in, as in **INSIDER TIP** Maroubra – before treating yourself to a cup of coffee in Pool Café opposite *(www.poolcafe.com.au)*. *Freshwater Beach* is a popular spot for surfers north of the resort of Manly. It is only 350m long, but the waves are up to 1.6m (over 5ft) high.

ENTERTAINMENT

BARS & PUBS

The most typical watering holes are in *The Rocks*. *The Australian (100 Cumberland Street)* and *The Lord Nelson (19 Kent Street)* and *The Argyle (12 Argyle Street)* have remained unspoilt, the first two also serving their own delicious home-brewed beer. *Establishment Bar* (U B3) *(ꟷ b3)* is a hotspot located on the ground floor of the boutique hotel of the same name.

248–252 George Street | Mon–Sat 11am–approx. 4am | Circular Quay. Vivaz (U B2) *(ꟷ b2)*: Get your body moving to the live music in this smart club and restaurant – samba, salsa, merengue, lambada, kambo or cumbia are the most popular dances. *80 George Street | www.vivaz.net.au | live music Fri/Sat from 10pm | Circular Quay*

DISCOS

Nightlife centres on *Oxford Street* and the neighbouring districts of *Paddington* and *Kings Cross*. Clubs often open until around 5am at weekends include *Kinselas (383 Bourke Street | bus 389)*, *Sugareef (20 Bayswater Road | bus 326 to Kings Cross)*, *Oxford Hotel (134 Oxford Street | bus 333)*.

CASINO

Star City (0) *(ꟷ 0)*: Impressive casino with pretty fountains in the foyer and a

Bars and pubs in Sydney's oldest district, The Rocks

shopping arcade. *80 Pyrmont Street | www.starcity.com.au | Monorail*

OPEN-AIR CINEMA

Australians love open-air cinemas. In Sydney these are *St George Open Air Cinema* in the Royal Botanic Garden at *Mrs. Macquarie's Chair (Jan/Feb, A$23, www.stgeorgeopenair.com.au)*, *Moonlight Cinema* in *Centennial Park (Jan–March, A$15, www.moonlight.com.au)*, *Bondi Openair Cinema* on the beach promenade with music played beforehand *(Jan–March, A$18) www.bondiopenair.com.au)*.

THEATRE & OPERA

Company B/Belvoir Street Theatre (0) *(* 0)*: Australia's leading theatre company that produced the likes of Mel Gibson. *25 Belvoir Street | tel. 02 96 99 34 44 | www.belvoir.com.au*

Sydney Theatre Company (U B2) *(* b2)*: Cate Blanchett heads this highly professional troupe of actors. The ambitious list of plays performed can be found under *www.sydneytheatre.com.au (tel. 02 92 50 19 99 | Pier 4/5, The Rocks)*.

Theatre Royal (U B4) *(* b4)*: Folk as well as experimental theatre and comedy. *MLC Center | Pitt Street/King Street/Martin Place | tel. 02 92 24 84 44 | Martin Place*

Wharf Theatre (0) *(* 0)*: (Dance) theatre in the former Walsh Bay shipyard. Mostly mainstream, rarely classics. *Pier 4–5 Hickson Road, Millers Point | tel. 02 92 50 17 77*

WHERE TO STAY

QUAY WEST SUITES SYDNEY
(U B1) *(* b1)*

Luxury hotel with view of the harbour and a wonderful 'Roman' pool. *121 rooms | 98 Gloucester Street | tel. 02 92 40 60 00 | www.mirvac.com.au | Expensive | within walking distance of Circular Quay*

INSIDER TIP OLD SYDNEY HOLIDAY INN
(U B2) *(* b2)*

Atrium hotel in the middle of The Rocks; some of the rooms are a bit small but some have a view of the Opera House and Harbour Bridge. The view from the roof-top pool open to all guests however is simply unbeatable. *175 rooms | 55 George Street | tel. 02 92 52 05 24 | www.ichotelsgroup.com | Expensive | Circular Quay*

SYDNEY HARBOUR YOUTH HOSTEL
(U B1) *(* b1)*

Expensive as far as youth hostels go, but good value considering the view of the harbour and Opera House. You're more or less sleeping 'under the bridge' – the Sydney Harbour Bridge, that is – and are slap bang in the middle of the Old Town district of The Rocks. The best views are to be had from the ☆ roof terrace. Booked out ages in advance so plan your stay early! *106 rooms | 110 Cumberland Street | tel. 02 82 72 09 00 | www.yha.com.au | Budget–Moderate | Circular Quay*

VICTORIA COURT HOTEL
(0) (*☐ 0*)
Romantic, small and exquisite. The best rooms in this hotel have marble fireplaces, huge mirrors and glittering chandeliers. *25 rooms | 122 Victoria Street | tel. 02 93 57 32 00 | www.victoriacourt.com.au | Moderate | bus 389*

INSIDER TIP▶ Y ON THE PARK
(0) (*☐ 0*)
The insider tip to beat all tips – very clean accommodation not only for backpackers

but also for families. *150 rooms | 5–11 Wentworth Ave. | tel. 02 92 64 24 51 | www.yhotel.com.au | Budget–Moderate | bus 389*

INFORMATION

SYDNEY VISITOR CENTRE
(U B2) (*☐ b2*)
Argyle/Playfair Street, The Rocks Centre | tel. 02 92 40 87 88 | www.seesydney.com.au

WHERE TO GO

BLUE MOUNTAINS NATIONAL PARK ★
(177 D5–6) (*☐ H6*)
The wild Blue Mountains start 110km (68mi) west of Sydney. The *Three Sisters*, an impressive rock formation near the little town of *Katoomba*, are of considerable spiritual importance to the local Aborigines. Wonderful views over deep gorges and the forested mountain ranges in the national park can be had from ☆ *Echo Point* not far from the spectacular *Three Sisters*.

Just a few hundred yards away on the western outskirts of Katoomba, ☆ *Scenic World* combines breath-taking views with a bit of excitement. The more daring can take the *Scenic Railway* that plunges 415m (1362ft) down a steep incline, then the *Scenic Skyway,* a cablecar across the gorge far below, the *Scenic Cableway,* another cablecar ride up or down and hike along the well-maintained 3km (2½mi)-long *Scenic Walkway* through the rainforest *(daily 9am–5pm | www.scenicworld.com.au | A$28 for the all-inclusive Scenic Pass).*

You can stay in the stylish *Hydro Majestic (115 rooms | Medlow Bath | Great Western Highway | www.hydromajestic.com.au | Expensive)* or in one of the ten log cabins at *Jemby-Rinjah Eco Lodge* in the heart

LOW BUDGET

▶ If the *Bridge Climb* in Sydney is too expensive for you, then you can still enjoy a spectacular view of the city, the harbour and Opera House for just 11 A$ from the *Pylon Lookout*. It can be reached via the pedestrian pathway from The Rocks *(Bridge Stairs | Cumberland Street | daily 10am–5pm | www.pylonlookout.com.au).*

▶ The Blue Mountains Explorer Pass (Link Ticket) that will take you from Circular Quay to the heart of the Blue Mountains, is valid for three days and costs just A$67. From there, the Blue Mountains Explorer Bus stops at 30 sights. Tickets available on Circular Quay *(www.cityrail.info)* and elsewhere.

of the bush, *336 Evans Lookout Road | Blackheath | tel. 02 47 87 76 22 | www.jembyrinjahlodge.com.au | Moderate–Expensive*. Information, maps and books available from the *NPWS Blue Mountains Heritage Centre (Govetts Leap Road | Blackheath | tel. 02 47 87 88 77 | www.visitbluemountains.com.au)*. Various bus *Visitor Centre* a route leads you through parks and gardens to the most interesting buildings. If you want a break from all the walking, take your bathing things with you and cool off in one of the many pools in the *Sydney Aquatic Centre. Visitor Centre | Herb Elliot Avenue | www.sydneyolympicpark.com.au | daily 9am–5pm*

You will seldom be on your own here: a viewpoint in the Blue Mountains

companies run day-trips from Sydney. Trains run from *Central Station (www.cityrail.info)* and connect with the Katoomba Trolley Bus *(www.trolleytours.com.au)* that stops at the major sights.

HOMEBUSH BAY (177 E5) (*ⓜ J6*)
The best way to reach the Olympic Park in Homebush Bay, 14km (8½mi) away, is to take the River Cat Ferry from Circular Quay Wharf 5. From the *Olympic Park*

HUNTER VALLEY
(177 E5) (*ⓜ H–J6*)
The Hunter Valley, some 160km (100mi) north of Sydney, is the oldest wine-growing region in Australia with more than 50 excellent wineries *(www.winecountry.com.au)*, producing delicate, fruity white wines and some reds (Pinot Noir and Shiraz). Many wineries also have first-class restaurants – and luxurious accommodation for overnight stays.

NEW SOUTH WALES

Endless beaches, eucalyptus forests around romantic lakes, isolated farms and cattle stations, huge national parks from the desert to the rainforest, subtropical heat and freezing temperatures in the Snowy Mountains – all this is New South Wales.

The 'First State' *(www.visitnsw.com)*, at 309,500mi² more than 3 times the size of the UK, is the oldest and most densely populated state in Australia – although outside Sydney with its population of 4½ million you don't really notice this. There are lots of empty beaches along its 1000km (620mi)-long coastline, you can hike for days in the Snowy Mountains without ever meeting a soul, and in the pubs in the outback strangers are still something of a novelty. However, for many visitors who land at Sydney airport, the fascinating state capital overshadows the 'rest' of New South Wales.

BATEMANS BAY

(179 F1) *(Ø H7)* **A friendly place (pop. 13,000) at the estuary of the Clyde River.** Some 240km (150mi) south of Sydney, it is a good starting point for exploring the

---

Sea, forests, mountains and desert: the state of New South Wales is moving out of the shadow cast by its capital Sydney

hidden beaches, fishing villages and national parks along the South Coast.

SIGHTSEEING

MURRAMURANG NATIONAL PARK
The national park runs down a spectacular stretch of coast with small sandy beaches, steep cliffs and numerous caves. Hikers and fossil hunters in particular will find what they are looking for here. At Pebbly Beach, so-called mobs of seemingly tame kangaroos can be seen grazing.

FOOD & DRINK

STARFISH DELI
Fish and pizza restaurant right on the water. *Clyde Street | tel. 02 44 72 48 80 | open every day | Budget*

BATEMANS BAY

WHERE TO STAY

CHALET SUISSE SPA
B&B with a view of the sea, spring water, swimming pool, massages, aromatherapy.
18 rooms | 676 The Ridge Road | tel. 02 44 71 36 71 | www.chaletswissespa.com.au |
Expensive

INFORMATION

BATEMANS BAY VISITOR CENTRE
Princes Highway | tel. 02 44 72 69 00 | www.southcoast.com.au

Crystal-clear water:
Jervis Bay National Park

WHERE TO GO

JERVIS BAY NATIONAL PARK
(177 D–E6) (*ΦΩ H6-7*)
The park is some 100km (62mi) north of Batemans Bay and comprises heathland, eucalyptus forests and small pockets of rainforest. Kangaroos, wallabies and flying foxes can be seen almost everywhere. Parrots land on the arms and shoulders of anyone who has bird food with them. Dolphins and penguins live in the sheltered bays with brilliant white beaches and crystal-clear water. In winter, whale-watching is possible *(Dolphin Watch Cruises | 50 Owen Street, Huskisson | from A$27 | tel. 02 44 41 63 11 | www.dolphin watch.com.au)*.

KIAMA
(177 E6) (*ΦΩ H6*)
The pretty historical part of this town (pop. 11,000) 130km (80mi) north of Batemans Bay, follows the rugged cliffs along the coast to *Blowhole*, Kiama's special attraction. When the wind comes from the southwest, the waves crashing against the cliffs are forced through a deep underwater cavern and shoot 60m (200ft) up through a hole in the rock.

SNOWY MOUNTAINS
(179 E1–2) (*ΦΩ H7*)
The mountains rising above the south coast are only ever visited by a few foreign tourists. The Snowies however are not just a magnet for winter sports enthusiasts. In summer, you can experience the solitude of the mountains in this huge national park such as can no longer be found in Europe. A large part of the 'Australian Alps' that stretch as far as Victoria, is a protected area – in New South Wales as the *Mount Kosciuszko National Park*, in Victoria the *Alpine National Park*. In 2003 and 2006 forest fires caused considerable

damage to the region. The tourist centres are *Cooma, Thredbo* and *Jindabyne.*
An unforgettable experience is a ride through the outlying areas of the national park over a period of several days. Information: *Snowy Mountains Tourist Information | Cooma | 119 Sharp St. | tel. 02 64 50 17 42 | www.snowymountains.com. au* and *www.nationalparks.nsw.gov.au*

BROKEN HILL

(175 E4) *(𝄞 G6)* **When driving along the highway the town (pop. 19,000) suddenly appears out of nowhere: an urban oasis in a desert-like environment.**
There are a number of hotels, restaurants and all sorts of shops in the centre and a respectable cultural scene, as well as any amount of precious metal below ground. Zinc, lead and silver were discovered here back in 1885. One of the largest mines operated by the *Broken Hill Proprietary Company (BHP)*, that grew to become one of the biggest in the world, was established in this range of hills that appeared to have a break in it – hence the name. Despite intensive mining, the reserves have no where nearly been exhausted. But *The Silver City*, as the town is famously called, is wary of the future and is therefore putting its money on tourism: remarkable attractions (incl. a very interesting flying doctor base) and other sights now make the long journey inland worthwhile. Here, by the way, you'll have to adjust your watch. Although the town is in New South Wales, it is in the South Australian time zone.

Historic Junction Mine in Broken Hill

gives an impression of the hard and dangerous work in the mine at the end of the 19th century when even children were sent underground. *20km (12½mi) northwest, turning signposted off the road to Silverton | Easter–Nov daily 10am–3.30pm, Dec–Easter daily 10am and 11.30am | A$20*

LINE OF LODE MINERS MEMORIAL
This memorial to the hundreds of workers who died in the mine is in a fitting location on Federation Hill above the town. Good views, an informative visitor centre

⭐ **Byron Bay**
Not only loved by watersports enthusiasts: sun, sand and surf – and wonderful scenery → p. 50

⭐ **Koala Hospital**
Marsupials on the mend: this is where vets show loving care for injured koalas → p. 54

MARCO POLO HIGHLIGHTS

SIGHTSEEING

DAY DREAM SILVER MINE
A 1-hour guided tour (sturdy shoes necessary) through the narrow, low galleries

and a meeting place for gourmet's *(Broken Earth Café & Restaurant | tel. 08 80 87 13 18, reservations essential! | Moderate–Expensive)*.

and the unconventional artist studios which have been set up in the deserted buildings and are well worth a visit. Your walk through this dusty place should also

Mad Max was here too, but he didn't spend the night in Silverton

SCULPTURE SITE

This modern sculpture park is out in the desert, at the top of a hill and far enough from the lights of the town to show off the colours to their best especially at sunrise or sunset. 20 mins. from the carpark. A map and a key for the gate to the drive can be obtained for a small fee from the visitor centre.

INSIDER TIP SILVERTON

A bizarre ghost town from the days when silver was mined on a grand scale, 24km (15mi) northwest. However, you will still meet people here in the little-changed pub *(Silverton Hotel, basic rooms | tel. 08 80 88 53 13 | Budget)*, in the small café

include the old cemetery. Silverton, incidentally, is well known in the Australian film industry. This picturesque outback post has often formed the backdrop for cinema productions such as *Mad Max II* and *Priscilla, Queen of the Desert.*

FOOD & DRINK

BELLS

The retro milk bar has survived since the 1950s and unflinchingly continues to serve all sorts of flavours of non-alcoholic milkshakes and soda spiders. *160 Patton Street, in the south of the town | tel. 08 80 87 53 80 | www.bellsmilkbar.com.au | daily 10am–5.30pm*

SHOPPING

INSIDER TIP ARTS AND CRAFTS

There are any number of *Art Galleries* and *Craft Shops* in Broken Hill and you can spend days visiting studios and exhibitions here. A list of addresses and contacts is available from the visitor centre. Howard W. Steer's dazzlingly paintings are typical and now fetch high prices *(www.howard-steerart.com.au).* Pro Hart Gallery exhibits (and sells) works by the local artist Kevin Charles Hart who died a few years ago *(108 Wyman Street | www.prohart.com. au | Mon–Sat 9am–5pm | A$4).*

WHERE TO STAY

THE LODGE OUTBACK MOTEL

Quietly and centrally located; all rooms on the ground floor; friendly host. *252 Mica Street | tel. 08 80 88 27 22 | www. lodgemotel.com.au | Moderate*

ROYAL EXCHANGE HOTEL

Art Deco on the outside, tastefully renovated and comfortable accommodation inside; in the centre. *320 Argent Street | tel. 1800 67 01 60 or 08 80 87 23 08 | www. RoyalExchangeHotel.com | Moderate–Expensive*

INFORMATION

VISITOR INFORMATION CENTRE

Blende/Bromide Street | tel. 08 80 80 35 60 | www.visitbrokenhill.com.au

WHERE TO GO

MUTAWINTJI NATIONAL PARK

(175 E–F3) *(*ϖ *G5)*

In this park that covers 266mi², 130km (80mi) northeast of Broken Hill, there are a number of intriguing cave paintings and especially engravings by Aborigines who once lived here. Background information is available in the *Cultural Centre.* It can be reached along an unmade road and you can stay on *Homestead Campground* which has a small shop *(no reservations | tel. 08 80 80 32 00 | www.nationalparks. nsw.gov.au).* A guided day-trip in a 4×4 from Broken Hill can be recommended *(Tri State Safaris | tel. 08 80 88 23 89 | www. tristate.com.au, A$180).*

INSIDER TIP WHITE CLIFFS

(175 F3) *(*ϖ *G5)*

Opal seekers have turned this area 290km (180mi) northeast of Broken Hill into a lunar landscape where life is largely spent underground in the cool and shade. And this is how you can stay in the *White Cliffs Underground Motel* with restaurant *(31 rooms | tel. 08 80 91 66 77 | www.under groundmotel.com.au | Moderate)*, in the earth and without a window – but quite

largely younger, well-heeled tourists who really get things going in the evenings on Bay Street along the waterfront, while during the day surfers enjoy the incredibly wide and beautiful beaches. *Main Beach* stretches 50km (31mi) almost as far as

The lighthouse on Cape Byron has one of the most powerful beams in the southern hemisphere

cosily. Bathrooms are shared with other guests. Imaginatively designed opal jewellery is available from the goldsmith Barbara Gasch *(Dugout 142)*.

the Gold Coast in Queensland, whereas *Watego's Beach* is a dream-come-true for surfers who ride the long breakers alongside dolphins for all their worth.

BYRON BAY

(177 F2) *(∅ J5)* ★ **With all sorts of water sports, a fantastically beautiful hinterland and high mountains and a lively pub scene, Byron Bay (pop. 9000) is a booming tourist destination.**

This was once the preserve of backpackers and dropouts – but they have long since moved further inland to Nimbin. It is

SIGHTSEEING

CAPE BYRON

This peninsula, named by James Cook on his first trip (1768–71), juts out a long way into the sea. You can drive to the old lighthouse or take the path to *Captain Cook Lookout* (3.5km/2mi). From here you have an overwhelming view of Watego's Bay. June/July and Sept–Nov is the best time for whale-watching.

FOOD & DRINK

FINS
Fish and fun is the motto here: this very stylish restaurant is where local trendsetters like to be seen. *The Beach Hotel | Bay St. | tel. 02 66 85 50 29 | open every day | Expensive*

WHERE TO STAY

THE ARTS FACTORY BACKPACKERS LODGE
Out-of-the-ordinary accommodation (in tipis, five-sided log cabins, hammocks on an artificial island, a tent and a pretty cottage). *Skinners Shoot Road | tel. 02 66 85 77 09 | www.artsfactory.com.au | Budget–Moderate*

BYRON AT BYRON RESORT
Extensive terraces, cane furniture, small water features in the garden – the Resort is pure bliss in the heart of the rainforest some 5 mins. from Byron Bay. *92 rooms | 77 Broken Head Road | tel. 02 66 39 20 00 | www.thebyronatbyron.com.au | Expensive* Information

BYRON VISITOR CENTRE
80 Jonson Street | tel. 02 66 85 80 50 | www.visitbyronbay.com

WHERE TO GO

DORRIGO NATIONAL PARK
(177 E3) *(∅ J5)*
The park is 900m (2950ft) up in the mountains of the Great Dividing Range, 250km (155mi) south of Byron Bay. It is one of the most beautiful and accessible national parks in New South Wales. The 70m (230ft)-high skywalk, a 250m (820ft)-long path through the tree canopy of the rainforest can be especially recommended *(Dorrigo Rainforest Centre | daily 9am–5pm | Dome Road | www.dorrigo.com)*. Accommodation can be found in neighbouring Bellingen *(www.bellingen.com)* in Rivendell B&B *(4 rooms | 10 Hyde St. | tel. 02 66 55 00 60 | www.rivendellguesthouse.com.au | Budget)*. A number of artists, craftspeople and organic farmers have settled in and around this pretty historical village (pop. 2700). Good craft shops and a nice café can be found in the *Bellingen Butter Factory (2 Doepel Street)*.

MURWILLUMBAH AND MOUNT WARNING (177 F2) *(∅ J5)*
The area inland from Byron Bay, with banana plantations, dense rainforest and small villages with a colourful mixture of unconventional shops, is fascinating. From Byron Bay, head first of all for *Mullumbimby*,

MUNGO NATIONAL PARK

The Mungo National Park in the southwest of New South Wales, approx. 420km (260mi) northeast of Adelaide, covers some 108mi². According to experts, this could be the site of the cradle of humanity. The remains of animals long since extinct and prehistoric man show that the area has been used for tens of thousands of years. Some fossils are more than 40,000 years old, other estimates even suggesting 60,000 years old. These also include the remains of Mungo Man, named after the archaeological site, that are among the oldest bones of Homo sapiens anywhere.

The most expensive building in Australia: Parliament House in Canberra

then take the highway to *Murwillumbah (approx. 50km/31mi)*. From here, the roads to *Uki, Nimbin, Lismore* and the little artists' colony *Bangalow* are narrow and twisty. The turning to *Mount Warning National Park* is between Murwillumbah and Uki. ☀ *Mount Warning* is the remnant of a huge volcano that erupted millions of years ago. A unique ecological niche was created between the lava masses where wonderful rainforest and rare flora and fauna now thrive. It is well worth climbing Mount Warning INSIDERTIP early in the morning (approx. 2 hrs.) when the sun starts to rise above Australia's eastern-most point and the surrounding area is bathed in a fascinating light. Note: the final section should only be tackled if you have a head for heights. Sturdy shoes essential.

CANBERRA

(177 D6) (𝄞 H7) Canberra (population 330,000) is the result of a compromise between Sydney and Melbourne after they could not agree on which city should become the capital.

It was literally built in the middle of no-where. 'Canberry' – the meeting place – was what the Aborigines called the area. The American architects Walter Burley Griffin and Marion Mahony Griffin won the commission to build the city in 1912. Canberra is characterised by its strict geometrical design. The city itself and its suburbs cover about one third of the 930mi² of the total area in the Australian Capital Territory (ATC). Canberra has two hearts: the northern district around

culture of Australia. Subjects range from the history of the Aborigine people to the importance of Vegemite in contemporary Australia. *Lawson Crescent, Acton Peninsula | daily 9am–5pm | admission free | www.nma.gov.au*

PARLIAMENT HOUSE ●
This building is the seat of both national parliaments, the House of Representatives (Green Chamber) and the Senate (Red Chamber). The 81m (266ft)-high flagpole on the roof has become a symbol of the city of Canberra. The building cost 1.1 billion A$ and is the most expensive ever erected in Australia. It was inaugurated in 1988. More than 3000 works of art are on display in Parliament House, many of which are in rooms open to the public. Free guided tours can be booked on arrival. A visit is particularly interesting when Question Time is being held in parliament. Verbal attacks and rude remarks between the Government and the Opposition are not unusual. For information on the days parliament sits and opening times: *tel. 02 62 77 48 99 | www.aph.gov.au*

London Circuit and the southern one around *Capital Hill,* where parliament stands. A trip to ☀ *Mount Ainslie Lookout* provides the best picture of the city with the government district being particularly clear.

SIGHTSEEING

NATIONAL GALLERY OF AUSTRALIA
International art spanning a period of 5000 years and an exceptional collection of Aboriginal works, some of which date back 30,000 years, are on display here. *Parkes Place | daily 10am–5pm | admission free | www.nga.gov.au.*

NATIONAL MUSEUM OF AUSTRALIA
The museum provides an interesting insight into the history and multifaceted

FOOD & DRINK

BOAT HOUSE BY THE LAKE
Wonderful location on Lake Burley Griffin pared with excellent Australian cuisine *(main course approx. A$38). Grevillea Park (northern edge of Barton) | Menindee Drive | tel. 02 62 73 55 00 | www.boathousebythe lake.com.au | closed afternoons and Sun | Expensive*

SAMMY'S KITCHEN
Excellent Asian cooking in the city centre. Try the shan tung chicken. Reservations recommended. *Bunda Street | Garema Centre | tel. 02 62 47 14 64 | open every day | Moderate*

WHERE TO STAY

NOVOTEL

The hotel is just a few yards from a number of different restaurants. Cheaper at weekends. *197 rooms | 65 Northbourne Ave. | tel. 02 62 45 50 00 | www.novotel canberra.com.au | Moderate*

ENTERTAINMENT

A list of events can be found under *www. outincanberra.com.au.*

HIPPO LOUNGE BAR

This bar is famous for the best Martinis in town. The proprietors also have a soft-spot for good live jazz. Try the bar's own fruity cocktail creation, the *Jet Li. 17 Garema Place | Wed–Sun from around 5pm*

CANBERRA THEATRE

It also houses the little studio Playhouse Theatre and is focused on dramas, musicals and comedies. *London Circuit | tel. 02 62 57 10 71 or toll-free 1800 04 10 41 | www. canberratheatre.org.au*

INFORMATION

CANBERRA VISITORS CENTRE

Northbourne Avenue | tel. 02 62 05 00 44 | www.visitcanberra.com.au

PORT MACQUARIE

(177 F4) (*[U] J6*) Fondly called 'Port' by the locals, the town (pop. 40,000) on the estuary of the Hastings River was founded by convicts in 1821 and is one of the oldest settlements in Australia.
Port Macquarie offers all sorts of water sports activities as well as mile-long beaches for swimming or surfing, stretching from *Town Beach* and *Oxley Beach* near the town centre to *Lighthouse Beach* in the south.

SIGHTSEEING

OYSTER FARMS

A large percentage of the oysters sold in Australia are farmed in the waters of Port Macquarie. Some tours stops at the oyster farms, e.g. the *Port Macquarie Cruise Adventures/Waterbus Evergladers Tour | Short Street Town Wharf | tel. 02 65 83 84 83 | tel. 1300 55 58 90.*

KOALA HOSPITAL ★ ●

The largest animal clinic of its kind in Australia is run on an honorary basis and often has more than 30 patients. The marsupials taken in here are often the victim of a road accident or bush fire. After being treated by expert vets and when they have fully recovered, they are released back into the wild. They are fed daily at 3pm. *Lord Street | daily 9am–5pm | admission free, donations gratefully received | www.koalahilfe.de | www.koala hospital.org.au*

SEA ACRES RAINFOREST CENTRE

The 1.3km (¾mi) board walk – supposedly the longest in the world – and up to 7m (23ft) over the ground, takes you through an unspoilt tropical rainforest. Displays illustrate how the second largest rainforest in New South Wales evolved. *Sea Acres Nature Reserve | Pacific Drive 6 km (3¾mi) north of the town centre | daily 9am–4.30pm | A$22*

FOOD & DRINK

PORT MACQUARIE FISH MARKET

This is where you can find cheap fresh oysters, among other delicacies. *Clarence

*Street | on the harbour | Mon–Fri 8am–
6.30pm, Sat 4.30pm, Sun 4pm*

WHERE TO STAY

SAILS RESORT

The best hotel in the area with a very good restaurant is situated right on the water a little outside the town but near a shopping centre. *83 rooms | Park Street | tel. 02 65 83 39 99 | www.sailsresort.com.au | Moderate–Expensive*

WHERE TO GO

KEMPSEY
(177 F4) (*Ⓜ J6*)

Since 1974 all Akubra hats made in Australia have come from this little town (pop. 11,000) 40km (25mi) north of Port Macquarie. They have to be indestructable and be able to cope with the rain and sun as well as frost. The felt is made from rabbit fur, with only the animal's soft undercoat being used. The name Akubra is

'Say cheese': no more koalas could fit on this branch

SUNDOWNER BREAKWALL TOURIST PARK

Near the town and right on the beach but in a very sunny spot. *22 cabins and flats | 1 Munster Street | tel. 02 65 83 27 55 | www. sundownerholidays.com | Budget*

INFORMATION

VISITOR INFORMATION CENTRE
Gordon St. corner Gore St. | tel. 02 65 81 80 00 | www.portmacquarieinfo.com.au

from the Aborigine language and means 'headgear'.

Unfortunately the only factory in the town is not open to the public. However, in the *Kempsey Visitor Information (Pacific Highway/South Kempsey Park | tel. 02 65 63 15 55 | www.macleayvalleycoast.com. au)*, you can watch a 15-min. video every day between 9am–5pm on how the hats are produced and then go and select an Akubra for yourself in one of a number of shops.

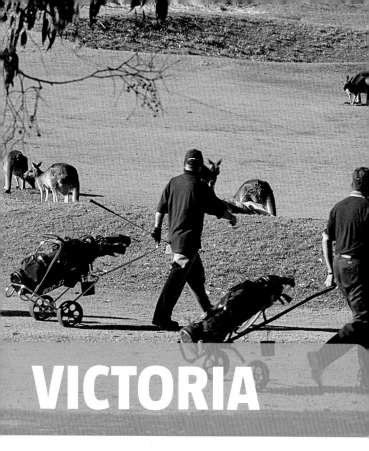

VICTORIA

Covering some 88,000mi², Victoria is the second smallest state in Australia and yet it has the most diverse landscape. Although it is home to only 6 million people, it is in fact the most populated state.

Victoria has everything: a rugged coastline, endless beaches for surfing, swamps, agricultural land, snow-covered mountains and barren deserts. It was in Victoria that gold was first discovered in 1850. Tens of thousands of people descended on Melbourne as a result to try their luck in the nearby gold-fields and, today, the vast majority of Victorians – some 75% in fact – now live in Melbourne.

GRAMPIANS

(178 B2) (*ℳ G7*) **The jagged Grampian mountains tower 1000m (3280ft) up above the green pastureland 260km (162mi) west of Melbourne.**

Hidden gorges, clear rivers and spectacular waterfalls provide a home to a wide variety of plants and animals. For the local Aborigines, the mountains – that they call *Gariwerd* – are of great spiritual importance, as numerous rock art sites testify. These are best explored with a guide. In the INSIDER TIP *Brambuk Aboriginal Cultural Centre* in the main centre *Halls*

Lively cultural scene, stunning scenery: Victoria has a breath-taking coastline, cultivated lifestyle and a bush-ranger past

Gap *(Dunkeld Road | www.brambuk.com. au)*, an exhibition explains the lives and Dreaming stories of the Aborigines from the area. Halls Gap (pop. 250) is also the best starting point for nature-lovers and extreme sports fans in the Grampians. Tired hikers can relax in the *Kookaburra* café restaurant *(Tue–Sun from noon | Main Rd. | tel. 03 53 56 42 22 | Moderate)*. The 25 cosy log cabins in *D'Altons Resort (Glen St. |* tel. *03 53 56 46 66 | www.daltonsresort. com.au | Moderate)* have ☼ verandah with wonderful views. There is also a youth hostel in Halls Gap: *Grampians YHA Eco-Hostel* is a friendly ecologically run hostel with 60 beds in 2 and 4-bed rooms *(Buckler St./Grampians Road | tel. 03 53 56 45 44 | www.yha.com.au | Budget)*. For information on the Grampians see: *www.visitgrampians.com.au*

Impressive architecture: Federation Square in the heart of Melbourne

WHERE TO START?
Federation Square is the perfect starting point for visitors as this is where the Information Centre and several interesting museums can be found, Flinders St. Station is on the other side and it's only a short walk across Princes Bridge to the Southbank complex with good restaurants, the casino and breath-taking views from Eureka Tower. It is also not far from the main shopping area around Swanson Street. If you don't want to walk, take the free City Circle tram which will take you comfortably to many of the sights. But whatever you do, don't try to drive into the centre. It's very difficult to find somewhere to park and the multi-storey carparks are incredibly expensive. Trains, trams and buses are a much better alternative.

MELBOURNE

MAP ON PAGE 61
(178–179 C–D 2–3) (G7) Melbourne is a microcosm. The whole world seems to have made its home here – or at least people from 140 nations.

The locals are proud of the fact that their 'City of Diversity' is home to the largest Greek community outside Greece and so it comes as no surprise that the menus in the more than 3000 restaurants in the city have simply everything on offer. What do you fancy today – Italian, Greek or perhaps Mongolian, Tibetan, Nepalese or Jamaican cuisine?

The streets laid out on a grid pattern are also a mixture of everything. Majestic Victorian buildings, such as those on *Collins Street*, rub shoulders with bold skyscrapers or modern shopping arcades made of glass and steel. In between, there are spacious landscaped parks such as the

Queen Victoria Gardens or the Royal Botanic Gardens. And a packed calendar of events ensures that the 4 million Melbournians don't get bored – this has even resulted in the metropolis becoming known as the 'City of Events'.

SIGHTSEEING

AQUARIUM

Deep sea fans can experience life in the ocean without getting their feet wet. Visitors pass through a Plexiglas tunnel in the underwater world. One attraction with a special kick is diving with the sharks in the aquarium. *Flinders/King St. | daily 9.30am–6pm, Jan 9pm | A$26 | www.melbourneaquarium.com.au*

COOK'S COTTAGE

The house in England where the parents of James Cook, who discovered Australia, once lived was dismantled stone by stone and shipped in 2000 sections around the world to Melbourne, where it was rebuilt exactly as it was before, in the middle of a park. An impressive show of respect for the colonial seafarer whose life work is documented inside. *Fitzroy Gardens | daily 9am–5pm | A$5*

EUREKA SKYDECK 88

The lift shoots you to the 88th floor in just 40 seconds, 300m (985ft) up. The windows on all sides open up a breath-taking 360° panorama right over the other skyscrapers in Melbourne. You get the feeling of walking on thin air if you dare to step into 'The Edge' – a fully glazed projecting bay. *Riverside Quay Southbank | daily 10am–10pm | www.eurekaskydeck.com.au | from A$18*

FEDERATION SQUARE ★

The huge, modern museum and restaurant complex right on the banks of the Yarra, opposite Flinders St. Station, was built to commemorate the 100th anniversary of the State of Victoria. The pointed, slanting, glazed, zinc-clad building houses the largest holdings of Australian art, including an excellent collection of old and modern Aboriginal art and the National Gallery of Victoria Collection. *Daily 11am–6pm | admission free | www.fedsq.com*

GOLDEN MILE HERITAGE TRAIL

Most of the city's highlights can be reached on foot. The free *Official Melbourne Visitors' Map* is a great help – you only need to follow the Golden Mile Heritage Trail *(Golden Mile Booklet approx. A$8 | 2-hour guided tour daily 10am from Federation Square, approx. A$23 | tel. 13 00 78 00 45 | www.visitvictoria.com.au)*. It takes you through the most elegant streets in the centre and through China-

---

MARCO POLO HIGHLIGHTS

★ Federation Square
The largest collection of Australian art is housed in this controversial building
→ p. 59

★ Melbourne Museum
This is where you can find out about the history and culture of the Aborigines
→ p. 60

★ Royal Botanic Gardens
Sport, concerts and bats in Melbourne's 'green lung'
→ p. 60

★ Phillip Island
Tiny penguins in their best dress-coats march up the beach every evening
→ p. 66

town, past Victorian shopping arcades, theatres, several museums and the pompous *Royal Exhibition Building* and finishes at *Melbourne Museum.*

IMMIGRATION MUSEUM ●

Here you can experience for yourself the difficulties immigrants had to endure on their way to Australia. *400 Flinders St. | daily 10am–5pm | A$8*

MELBOURNE MUSEUM ★

The futuristic, interactive museum combines architecture and the natural environment – you can even walk through a wood in the middle of the museum. The Bunjilaka exhibition on the ground floor is an excellent introduction to the spiritual, cultural and political history past and present of Australia's native inhabitants. *Nicholson Street/Carlton Gardens | daily 10am–5pm | A$8*

OBSERVATION DECK ☼

You have a sensational view over Melbourne from the 88th floor of the *Eureka Tower* on the Southbank. In *The Edge*, a projecting bay 300m (985ft) up that can take up to 12 people, the glass changes from non-transparent to transparent at the flick of a switch – a dizzying surprise effect *(Riverside Quay | daily 10am–10pm | www.eurekaskydeck.com.au).*

OLD MELBOURNE GAOL ●

The dingy old prison conveys something of the harsh judicial system that was once operated in the former British colony of Victoria. Between 1845 and 1929, 135 people were executed here. The candle-light evening tours through the jail are spine-chilling *(Hangman's Night Tours | 4-times a week 7.30pm, summer 8.30pm). Russell Street/Mackenzie Street | www.old melbournegaol.com.au | City Circle Tram*

Extensive views can be had from the Observation Deck in Eureka Tower

to Russell St./Latrobe St. | daily 9am–5pm.
Tickets for the evening tour must be booked in advance through *Ticketek (tel. 13 28 49 | www.ticketek.com.au).*

ROYAL BOTANIC GARDENS ★ ●

The botanic garden on the shore of the Yarra covers more than 8½ acres and is the city's green gem with lakes, foot and cycle paths, more than 60,000 rare species of plant from all over the world, parrots, flying foxes, nocturnally active possums, shady avenues of trees, formal gardens and elegant tea rooms. In summer, there are open-air performances on the covered *Sydney Myer Music Bowl* stage.
The INSIDER TIP *Aboriginal Heritage Walk* is a special highlight. Koori guides tells visitors of their history and culture on a stroll around the botanic garden. They explain which plants and types of fruit can be eaten or used for medicinal purposes and how to prepare them. *Visitors Centre/ Observatory Gate | Birdwood Avenue | www.rbg.vic.gov.au | Thu/Fri 11am (duration approx. 90 mins.) | guided tour A$25 (book tours for Tue/Thu and on the first Sun in the month!)*

ST KILDA BEACH

The historical St Kilda beach resort is one of the liveliest places in Melbourne. The old pier and the Victorian lidos on the beach have been carefully renovated. On Sundays artists and craftspeople sell their products on the palm-lined esplanade *(www.esplanademarket.com).* There are hundreds of restaurants and cafés in the wide but busy streets as well as fortune tellers and shops selling garish retro fashions. The beach can be reached from the city centre by tram nos. 16 and 96 in around 15 mins.

SHRINE OF REMEMBRANCE
Erected in memory of soldiers from Victoria who fell in World War I, this temple-like structure is a must for every school child which means it can get pretty crowded inside, especially for the ceremonial act of remembrance which is held every 30 mins. Then it's better to go up onto the roof to enjoy the fantastic views in all directions over the treetops of the surrounding park. *Kings Domain, St Kilda Road | daily 10am–5pm, guided tours daily 11am and 2pm*

WILLIAMSTOWN
In this nostalgic port, the modern city of Melbourne seems miles away and yet it is within eyeshot on the far side of Port Philip. Those interested in history and the romantically inclined should definitely pay it a visit. The best way to get there is to take the boat across the Yarra River *(Williamstown Ferry | daily from Southgate | tel. 03 95 17 94 44 | www.williamstown ferries.com.au)*. The trip gives you a picture of the old and new dockland areas, and approaching Williamstown by water is how others would have seen it in the early 19th century when arriving on sailing ships at a time when the international port was supposed to have been expanded – until Melbourne grew in importance.

Many historic buildings line Nelson Place: modest houses have been preserved just as grander homes, old pubs and imposing civic buildings. These often house small shops or restaurants which are a welcome stop on any tour. Railway fans will be drawn to the *Railway Museum (Champion Road | Mon/Fri noon–4pm, Sat/Sun noon–5pm | A$5)* with its astonishing collection from the steam age.

FOOD & DRINK

CIRCA
In the middle of the clubbing district in St Kilda Beach is one of Melbourne's most stylish restaurants (in the designer hotel The Prince). The 5-course tasting menu can be highly recommended. *2 Acland St. | tel. 03 95 36 11 22 | open every day | Expensive*

COOKIE
Great Thai cooking, super bar atmosphere *(252 Swanston St., Curtin House 1st floor | tel. 03 96 63 76 60, www.cookiemelbourn australia.com.au | Moderate)*. The trendy disco Toff is on the 2nd floor and, outside on the roof, the INSIDER TIP *Rooftop Cinema* seating 175 (mostly on loungers) and a small burger bar operates from Dec–early April *(tel. 03 96 63 35 96 | ticket reservations 3pm–6pm | approx. A$18 | www. rooftopcinema.com.au)*.

DOCKLANDS

A modern district of extravagant steel and glass buildings has been created around Victoria Harbour on the western outskirts of the city. It is known both for its expensive flats as well as its popular restaurants, leads you to *Little Collins St.* that is especially interesting between the *Block Arcade* and *Russell St.* Nearby *(corner of Bourke St. Mall and Elizabeth St.)* is the city's oldest shopping centre, the *Royal Arcade* (for the best chocolate go to *Koko Black).*

The cafés in Block Arcade are perfect for a short break while shopping

some right on the water, such as Mecca Bah which serves spicy Moroccan food. *55 A New Quay Promenade, tel. 03 96 42 13 00, Moderate*

SHOPPING

Melbourne is perfect for shopping. Tip: start on *Flinders St.* opposite *Flinders St. Station* and head for *Degraves St.*, cross *Flinders Lane* and on to *Centre Place* (between *Flinders Lane* and *Collins St.).* Excellent coffee can be found everywhere too. Cross over *Collins St.* and head for the *Block Arcade* diagonally opposite which

Melbourne's most elegant street of shops is *Collins St. (www.collinsstreet.com.au).* More unusual shops in the various districts of the city are best explored on foot; e.g. in the *Swan St. Precinct* from Richmond Station, along *Church St.* (where tram no. 78 runs), in *Chapel St.* beyond South Yarra (Toorak St.). Or get off tram no. 86 on the corner of Gertrude/Brunswick St. and head off down Gertrude St. to Smith St. Beyond no. 377 (level with Johnston St.) you will find many interesting outlet stores (Adidas, Icebreaker, Timberland, etc.), as well as in *Fashion Station (Southern Cross Station, Spencer St.).*

MELBOURNE

MELBOURNE CENTRAL ●
More than just a shopping centre with some 180 shops, restaurants and boutiques that stock Australian labels such as *Coogi* and *R. M. Williams* (stylish outback fashions). The Central is an architectural work of art with a huge glass cone arching above the 100-year-old, brick Coop's Shot Tower. *Swanston St./La Trobe St.*

QUEEN VICTORIA MARKET
Mountains of shiny oranges and lemons, carefully built pyramids of apples and mangos, delicious cakes and croissants, stands selling sausages and Parma ham, hundreds of different types of cheese, freshly baked bread and the bitter-sweet aroma of espresso and Asian spices. Welcome to the more than 100-year-old Queen Victoria Market at the northern end of the city centre, corner Victoria/Elizabeth St. *Tue and Thu 6am–2pm, Fri 6am–6pm, Sat 6–5pm, Sun 9am–4pm | www.qvm.com.au*

ENTERTAINMENT

Ballet, classical concerts, theatre and opera are generally performed in the *Victorian Arts Centre*; reservations under *tel. 1300 18 21 83 | Mon–Fri 9am–5pm or www.ticketmaster.com.au*. Half-price, last-minute tickets (cash only) available on the day of a performance from *Halftix Kiosk (Melbourne Town Hall | Mon 10am–2pm, Tue–Fri 11am–18, Sat 10am–4pm)*.
Melbourne is *the* city for night owls. One of its centres is *Brunswick St*. The cosmopolitan, the whacky and the very different can be found in 'in' venues such as *Bar*

Beautiful beach, beautiful sight: Apollo Bay on Great Ocean Road

Open (317 Brunswick St. | daily noon–2am) and *Kodiak Club (no. 272 | Wed–Sun from 5pm)*. The whole of *South Yarra* with its many trendy cafés, bars and discos is also popular – especially Chapel St. *Docklands*, Melbourne's new residential district around the former port, easily reached on the City Circle tram, is also a popular place for going out. All performances and events etc. can be found under *www.beat.com.au*, the online version of Melbourne's largest street paper.

WHERE TO STAY

CLARION SUITES GATEWAY

Lovely hotel with spacious flats, centrally located. The rooms with a view of the river (from the 7th floor upwards, also much quieter) take in the Yarra River and

lively Southgate with its many restaurants. *120 flats | 1 William St. | tel. 03 92 96 88 88 | www.clarionsuitesgateway.com. au | Moderate–Expensive*

THE LINDRUM

Classical boutique hotel right in the centre, diagonally opposite where the free City Circle line stops. *59 rooms | 26 Flinders St. | tel. 96 68 11 11 | www.hotellindrum. com.au | Expensive*

TRAVELODGE

Good, standard-category hotel on the Southbank next to Eureka Tower. 275 rooms with kitchenette, TV and Internet. *Southgate Avenue/Riverside Quay | tel. 03 86 96 96 00 | www.travelodge.com.au | Moderate*

INFORMATION

MELBOURNE VISITOR INFORMATION CENTRE

Federation Square | Flinders St. corner Russell St. | tel. 03 96 58 99 55 | www. visitvictoria.com | www.visitmelbourne. com/de | www.thatsmelbourne.com.au

WHERE TO GO

INSIDER TIP▸ APOLLO BAY
(178 C3) (*∅ G7*)

This pretty fishing village (pop. 2500) some 130km (80mi) southwest of Melbourne with a beach and a fascinating hinterland is perfect for the first longish stop along the *Great Ocean Road* (for more information see 'Trips & Tours', p. 132). Accommodation available at *Captain's at the Bay (21 Pascoe St. | tel. 03 52 37 67 71 | www. captains.net.au | Moderate)*. Modern Australian fare at *La Bimba (125 Great Ocean Road | tel. 03 52 37 74 11 | open every day | Moderate)*, especially fresh fish and crayfish.

BALLARAT GOLDFIELDS
(178 C2) (*G7*)

Gold, gold, gold! Those in search of gold, who fancy a ride in a stagecoach or want to see well-brought up ladies in pretty crinolines and big hats should definitely visit Ballarat (pop. 85,000), 110km (68mi) northwest of Melbourne *(www.ballarat. com)*. This is where the Australian gold rush began in 1851 and this is where some of the world's biggest gold nuggets have been found.

The Old Town with its bakeries, pubs, mineshafts and small school still exists today – in *Sovereign Hill*, a living museum on the edge of Ballarat. In the evening, the son et lumière 'Blood on the Southern Cross' recalls the brief uprising staged by the gold diggers against the British colonial government in 1854, the so-called *Eureka Stockade*, that was quashed in a bloody confrontation. *(Sovereign Hill Gold Mining Township | Main Road/Bradshaw Street | daily 10am–5pm | A\$43 | www. sovereighhill.com.au), son et lumière daily at varying times (A\$48 | reservation essential | tel. 03 53 32 97 40)*
Sovereign Hill Lodge (200 beds | Magpie St. | tel. 03 53 33 34 09 | www.sovereign hill.com.au | Budget–Expensive) right next to the Sovereign Hill Museum has accommodation in all price categories from dormitories to luxury suites furnished in the Victorian style.

PHILLIP ISLAND ★
(179 D3) (*G7*)

The island 140 km (87mi) south of Melbourne is connected by a bridge. Inviting beaches such as *Cape Woolamai Beach* are perfect for swimming or sunbathing. Tiny little fairy penguins can be watched returning to *Summerland Beach* every evening where they waddle in long lines back to their nests *(www.penguins.org. au)*. Penguin-watching is strictly regulated.

A serene picture: pleasure boats in the harbour at Port Fairy

Tickets *(A$22)* are available from the *Phillip Island Information Centre (www. visitphillipisland.com, www.visit basscoast. com)*, 1km (just over ½mi) after passing San Remo bridge, daily, times variable. Day-trips organised from Melbourne. Another attraction is the *Nobbies Centre* on the southwest point where the second largest seal colony in the world, comprising some 20,000 animals, can be seen – but only through high-tech cameras and on monitors. Boat tours available under *www. wildlifecoastcruises.com.au*

Holmwood Guesthouse B&B, a historical cottage near the beach, provides accommodation in the house and in two smaller anxiliary buildings. *6 rooms | 37 Chapel Street | Cowes | tel. 03 59 52 30 82 | www. holmwoodguesthouse.com.au | Moderate– Expensive*

PORT FAIRY
(178 B3) *(⍐ G7)*

This conservation village (pop. 4000) at the end of the Great Ocean Road is a wonderful place to unwind after your journey. *Oscars Waterfront Boutique Hotel (41 B Gipps St. | tel. 03 55 68 30 22 | www. oscarswaterfront.com | Expensive)* has 5 luxuriously and meticulously decorated double rooms with a view of the river and gardens surrounding this beautiful old villa. The *Victoria Hotel (Moderate)* serves modern Australian food and has 7 well-equipped flats for rent in sandstone cottages near the hotel. *42 Bank St. | tel. 03 55 68 28 91 | www.vichotelportfairy.com. au | Moderate*. Information: *Visitor Information Centre | 22 Bank St. | tel. 03 55 68 26 82 | www.greatoceanroad.org*

INSIDER TIP WILSONS PROMONTORY NATIONAL PARK (179 D3) *(⍐ H7)*

Wilsons Promontory is in Gippslands, some 200km (125mi) southeast of Melbourne (coast road to New South Wales) and is a paradise for wombats *(Norman Beach)*. The kangaroos, wallabies, possums, emus and koalas that also live here are largely active at dusk. Tiny gliders (pygmy possums) appear at night. Brightly-coloured parrots and thousands of waterfowl live

The gold rush lives on in Sovereign Hill Museum

in the eucalyptus forests and swamps in the river estuary. Dolphins, penguins and seals frolic around off the countless white beaches around the peninsula. In the national park itself, you can stay at *Tidal River* which has pitches for tents as well as flats and cabins (tel. *03 56 80 95 00 | Budget*). Food must be brought with you. Outside the park, accommodation is available in *Yanakie, Sandy Point, Waratah Bay, Walkerville* and *Foster*. Reservations and information under *www.promaccom. com.au.*

QUEENSLAND

Divers hover above the soft waving coral, huge Venus clams open their velvety green lips and sharks hunt thousands of brightly-coloured fish in turquoise lagoons between sharp coral formations. This offshore paradise that draws people from all over the world is, however, just one side of Queensland. The state has a number of other adventures in store too.

The ★ *Great Barrier Reef*, with its fascinating undersea world that runs for more than 2300km (1500mi) down the east coast of Australia, is Queensland's main attraction. It comprises more than 3000 individual reefs and more than 2000 tropical islands. The reef stretches from just above Bundaberg to its northernmost tip at Cape York. But Queensland also has much more to offer. Perfect surfing on the Gold Coast, a life far from the madding crowd in the mountains inland, a vibrant, sub-tropical capital – Brisbane, fascinating Aborigine culture and unspoilt national parks in the adventure region of Cape York, huge stations with thousands of head of cattle, and mining settlements in the savannah and deserts of the outback. Queensland *(www.queensland-australia. eu)* is the second largest state in Australia, covering 656,500mi² and is almost 7 times the size of the UK – with a population of less than 5 million.

Photo: Great Barrier Reef

Coral reefs, rainforests and the outback: Queensland is Australia's holiday paradise

AIRLIE BEACH

(169 D2) *(∅ H3)* **Near Proserpine, a long way south of Townsville, a turning off the coast road leads to Airlie Beach (pop. 5000).**

Before you get there, massive billboards along Bruce Highway invite you to visit the Whitsunday Islands. Airlie Beach's zest for life is immediately obvious *(www.airlie beach.com.au)* and it is not just the range of watersports on offer that is extensive. The diving and snorkelling tours to the famous Whitsundays are certainly well worth the money. Later in the day, the younger crowd parties it away in the discos and pubs along the town's only main road – Airlie Beach Road – often spilling out into the open.

Hamilton Island

FOOD & DRINK

DEJA VU

The terrace offers a view over Airlie Beach and the sea, the food is modern Mediterranean style and represents good value for money. *Gold Orchid Drive (Waters Edge Resort) | tel. 07 49 48 43 09 | closed Mon/Tue | Moderate*

SPORTS & ACTIVITIES

FLIGHTS OVER THE REEF

After a sightseeing tour, the seaplanes operated by Air Whitsunday land along the reef so you can go snorkelling. *2½ hours A\$320 | tel. 07 49 46 91 11 | www.airwhitsunday.com.au*

TOURS OF THE ISLANDS

Day-trips to the reef with time to snorkel or trips to various island from A\$90 *(Three Island Discovery Cruise)* are organised by *Fantasea Cruises (11 Shute Harbour Road | tel. 07 49 46 58 11 | www.fantasea.com.au or www.seethewhitsundays.com).*

DIVING

Several diving schools offer trips or courses over a few days for beginners and experienced divers from around A\$300, e.g *Whitsunday Scuba/Dive Australia (tel. 07 49 46 10 67 | www.scubacentre.com.au).*

WHERE TO STAY

INSIDER TIP **AIRLIE WATERFRONT B&B**
3 air-conditioned, beautifully furnished suites and flats with ocean views – and a tropical breakfast on the veranda in the morning. *Broadwater Avenue/Mazlin Street | tel. 07 49 46 76 31 | www.airliewaterfrontbnb.com.au | Expensive*

CORAL SEA RESORT

Hotel with palms, swimming pool with a view of the Whitsundays. *77 rooms | 25 Ocean View Avenue | tel. 07 49 46 64 58 | www.coralsearesort.com | Moderate*

WHERE TO GO

Off the coast around Airlies Beach there are 74 tropical islands and lots of small islets that make up the Whitsunday Islands (169 D2) (* DU H3*). Only eight of them are inhabited. Some are purely holiday islands with hotel complexes and nightlife, others are protected national parks that can be visited on day-trips. Excursion boats can drop the romantically inclined and adventurous off for a night or a few days on one the many uninhabited islands. *Whitsunday Island*, the uninhabited main island, is a particularly attractive national park with mangrove swamps and the snow white, fine sandy *Whitehaven Beach*, the most beautiful beach in Queensland. *Lindeman, Long Island* and *South Molle Island* have places to stay. Information: *Tourism Whitsundays | Bruce Highway | Proserpine | tel. 07 49 45 37 11 | www.tourismwhitsundays.com or www.mywhitsunday.com*

DAYDREAM ISLAND
(169 D2) (*DU H3*)

This island seems to have been cut straight out of a catalogue of dream destinations: pure white coral beaches with palms waving in the breeze behind them, flower-filled gardens further inland below rainforest-clad slopes. Not surprisingly, this tiny island – just 1km (just over ½mi) long and 5km (3mi) from the mainland – is popular among day-trippers. The long sandy beach has club-like facilities including swimming pools, places to eat and all sorts of watersports equipment to hire. If you spend the night in the *Daydream*

Island Resort (122 rooms | tel. 07 49 48 84 88 | www.daydreamisland.com | Expensive), you can look forward to an open-air cinema session in the evening. *Ferry from Abel Point Marina (near Airlie Beach) or Hamilton Island*

HAMILTON ISLAND
(169 D2) (*DU H3*)

The largest of the Whitsundays is also the one with the best tourist infrastructure – that has both its advantages and disadvantages. You can jet to the island directly from Melbourne and Sydney (slightly more expensive that flights to Proserpine,

★ Great Barrier Reef
The attraction par excellence on the east coast: millions of brightly-coloured fish, dolphins, corals and tropical islands → p. 68

★ Fraser Island
Whales, dolphins and dingos live in the unbelievably blue waters and in the jungle of this huge sand island off the coast of Queensland → p. 76

★ Skyrail
Cabins glide over gorges and the canopy of the rainforest → p. 78

★ Tjapukai Cultural Centre
Culture, history and myths relating to the local Aborigines → p. 78

★ Daintree National Park and Cape Tribulation
Tropical rainforests, dream-like beaches and clowd-covered mountains → p. 81

MARCO POLO HIGHLIGHTS

but you get to your destination quicker); on the other hand the number of hotels results in noticeably crowded swimming pools and beaches. Ferries run regularly between Hamilton and other islands, some of which can be visited as part of a day-trip (*www.hamiltonisland.com.au*).

1000km (620mi) to the west of Airlie Beach. The *Outback at Isa Park* and the accompanying visitor centre provide an exceptionally good conglomeration of all the town's attractions and characteristics. The new underground tour through the ● *Hard Times Mine*, a 1.2km (¾mi)-long

Flying over the outback near the former mining town of Mount Isa

HAYMAN ISLAND (169 D2) (*ᗰ H3*)

A resort of superlatives offers every conceivable luxury on the northern-most island in the Whitsunday group and, in the ● spa, you can let yourself be pampered from head to toe. *Hayman Resort | 244 rooms | tel. 07 49 46 91 00 | www.hayman. com.au | Expensive*

MOUNT ISA (167 D2) (*ᗰ F3*)

One particular highlight awaits visitors to this authentic mining town (pop. 22,000)

gallery, is almost as good as the old tour of *Mount Isa Mines,* that had to be booked often weeks in advance. In the adjoining *Riversleigh Fossils Centre and Laboratory* you can see how fossils from the Riversleigh district Unesco World Heritage Site near Mount Isa are conserved. The Kalkadoon Aborigines also provide information on the culture of the former original inhabitants of the region around the town *(19 Marian St. | tel. 07 47 49 15 55 | www.out-backatisa.com.au | daily 8.30am–5pm).*

Excursion tip: with the *mail run* operated by *West Wing Aviation (www.westwing.com.au)* you can spend the whole day flying to isolated areas in the outback, calling in at a number of farms (but with only short stops in each case).

A trip to the INSIDER TIP *Lawn Hill National Park*, a tropical oasis with the possibility of swimming in *Lawn Hill Gorge*, is also appealing. Make sure you visit the *Riversleigh Fossil Fields* when there, one of the four most important fossil sites in the world with quite unique testimonies to the prehistoric animal world of Australia.

BRISBANE

MAP INSIDE BACK COVER
(177 F1) (*ᗰ J5*) **Until well into the 1980s Brisbane was not much more than a sleepy provincial stopping point where those on their way to the tropical north could stock up on things.**

Today, the city is a destination in its own right for holiday-makers from around the world. Promenades along Brisbane River, good shops, a wide range of cultural events,

---

first-class restaurants and the South Bank recreational district are all characteristic of this city that started life as a penal colony.

The discovery and extraction of ores in the neighbouring area and the arrival of immigrants from all over the globe helped make the city more important in the 1950s and '60s. The 'World Expo 88' also had a decisive influence of Brisbane's development into an international metropolis. Today, some 2 million people live in this, the third largest city in Australia and the capital of Queensland. In early 2011, the city was catastrophically hit by massive flooding.

SIGHTSEEING

LONE PINE KOALA SANCTUARY ●
Representatives of Australia's animal kingdom such as koalas, kangaroos, possums, emus, platypuses and wombats live in this extensive sanctuary that starts approx. 8km (5mi) southwest of the city centre. Lone Pine is the largest koala park in the world. *Fig Tree Pocket | Jesmond Rd. | daily 8.30am–5pm | A$30 | www.koala.net*

QUEENSLAND CULTURAL CENTRE, ART GALLERY AND MUSEUM
The colossal concrete complex on the south bank of the river and on both sides of Victoria Bridge in the South Bank Parklands cannot fail to impress: the *Art Gallery (Mon–Fri 10am–5pm, Sat/Sun 9am–5pm)*, with its high-quality works of Aboriginal art and European painting and sculpture shown in temporary exhibitions, comes as quite a surprise. Together with the Gallery of Modern Art (GoMA) it is the largest modern art gallery in Australia *(www.qag.qld.gov.au)*, whereas the *Museum (daily 9am–5pm)* has clear displays on the history and natural history of Queensland.

CITY **WHERE TO START?**
You can find your way about this clearly laid out city quickly. The real centre is **King George Square**: walk a few yards to the pedestrianised *Queen St. Mall* with its air-conditioned shopping centre and shady cafés, and then on to *Brisbane River,* to discover the city's sights from the bank. If you arrive by train, you will come into *Roma St. Station,* buses from all directions stop in the centre. Multi-storey carparks can be found in the *Myer Centre,* among other places.

SOUTH BANK PARKLANDS

Near the museums on the south bank of Brisbane River, the former site of the World Expo 88 covering 39½ acres has been turned into a superb leisure area *(best reached across Victoria or Goodwill Bridge)*. *Streets Beach*, an unusual lake for swimming, was laid out as a lagoon with an imported sandy beach and, from the *Wheel of Brisbane*, you can look across the skyline of Brisbane from a height of 60m (200ft). There are many restaurants and snack bars in the vicinity and a lifestyle market is held at weekends *(tel. 07 38 67 20 51 | www.visitsouth bank.com.au)*.

LOW BUDGET

▶ A good alternative to commercially-run campsites are the many, well-signed places to spend the night in the national parks that cost approx. A$7 per person *(www.epa. qld.gov.au)*. They are only equipped with the bare necessities, but there is always a WC and sometimes a shower.

▶ As a contrast to the generally expensive eateries, the surf club in Palm Cove has quite reasonable prices.

▶ In the (artificial) lagoon in Cairns, you can grill your own food free of charge on one of the generally clean BBQs. A perfect picnic in the town in pleasant surroundings.

▶ Lots of tips on how to save money can be found under *www.backpacking queensland.com*

FOOD & DRINK

Excellent restaurants are to be found at *Riverside Centre* and *Eagle St. Pier* as well as *Fortitude Valley* and in *New Farm (Merthyr Road/Brunswick Street)*. *Given Terrace* and *Caxton Street (Paddington)* as well as *Park Road (Milton)* are further addresses, as is *South Bank*.

ANISE

Very good French cuisine is served in this, the best winebar in town. *697 Brunswick Street | tel. 07 33 58 15 58 | closed Sun evenings/Mon afternoons | Moderate*

BREAKFAST CREEK HOTEL

Popular beer garden known for its massive steaks. *2 Kingsford Smith Drive | tel. 02 32 62 59 88 | open every day | Budget*

INSIDER TIP TUKKA

Pronounced 'takka', similar to 'tucker' – the colloquial expression for everything that makes up a meal. The very best 'bush food' is served here: innovative and, more importantly, typically Australian. *145 B Boundary St., West End | tel. 07 38 46 63 33 | closed afternoons Mon–Sat | Moderate*

SHOPPING

The main shopping drag is *Queen St. Mall* with the pleasant *Brisbane Arcade*. *Riverside Market* is more individual *(Sun 8am– 4pm, Eagle St. Pier)*.

ENTERTAINMENT

A number of good bars and nightclubs can be found in *Fortitude Valley* on *Ann St.*, e.g. *Monastery* (no. 621), *Beat Mega Club* (no. 677) and *GPO Hotel* (no. 740). Good live music (especially hip hop, jazz and rock) is played at *The Zoo (Wed–Sat | 711 Ann St.)*. The atmosphere in the *Downunder*

Garinbal Aborigine hand print in Carnarvon Gorge

Bar (Edward St., at Central Station below the backpacker hotel) is international.

WHERE TO STAY

HOTEL IBIS BRISBANE
Good, standard-category hotel located in the city centre. *218 rooms | 27–35 Turbot St. | tel. 07 32 37 23 33 | www.ibishotel. com | Moderate*

KOOKABURRA INN BACKPACKERS
Simple accommodation for the young and young at heart. *18 rooms | 41 Phillips St. | tel. 07 38 32 13 03 | www.kookaburra-inn.com.au | Budget*

RYDGES SOUTH BANK
Centrally located on South Bank, some rooms with a view of the river and the city centre. *305 rooms | 9 Glenelg Street |* *tel. 07 33 64 08 00 | www.rydges.com | Moderate–Expensive*

INFORMATION

BRISBANE TOURISM
Queen St. Mall Pavillon, opposite Wintergarden shopping centre | tel. 07 30 06 62 90 | www.ourbrisbane.com | www. brisbane-australia.com | www.visitbrisbane. com.au

WHERE TO GO

INSIDER TIP CARNARVON NATIONAL PARK (168 C5) (∅ H4)
The 750km (470mi) journey from Brisbane via Roma to Carnarvon Gorge is well worth it. Ancient species of plants have survived in the 200m (656ft)-deep gorge of the Carnarvon River. Sheer overhang-

ing cliffs conceal rock paintings and hand prints made by the Garinbal Aborigines on their hunt for food there thousands of years ago. Information: *Ranger Station (tel. 07 49 84 45 05 | www.epa.qld.gov. au)*. Campers have to register weeks in advance. One alternative is the *Carnarvon Gorge Wilderness Lodge*, 30 safari cabins, incl. meals and tours *(tel. 07 49 84 45 03 | www.carnarvon-gorge.com | Moderate–Expensive)*.

home to an extraordinary variety of plants and animals. *Fraser Island* can be explored on a guided tour or with your own 4×4 *(permit needed, www.qld.gov.au/ camping)*. Access to the island is either by plane or ferry from Hervey Bay or Rainbow Beach *(www.rainbow-beach.org)*. The rainforests and some 40 freshwater lakes can be reached along a sandy track. One of the most beautiful lakes with a snow-white beach is *Lake McKenzie. Kingfisher*

A good spot for a bit of whale-watching: Hervey on the Fraser Coast

FRASER COAST
(169 F5) (*ad* J4)

The Fraser Coast 300km (186mi) north of Brisbane is well known for two reasons. *Hervey Bay* is considered by experts to be an excellent place for whale-watching. ★ *Fraser Island* is also unique in the world: covering 710mi² it is the largest sand island on earth and became a Unesco World Heritage Site in 1992. The island is up to 240m (790ft) high and

Bay Resort (262 rooms | tel. 07 41 20 33 33 | www.kingfisherbay.com | Expensive) provides the best accommodation.
Hervey Bay on the mainland is largely known by whale-watchers *(www.whale-watching.com.au)*. Between August and October there are up to 3000 humpback whales in the waters off the coast. A number of different tours start from *Urangan Boat Harbour*. Information: *Hervey Bay Tourism (Urraween Road/Maryborough*

Rd. | tel. 07 41 24 29 12 | www.hervey.com. au, www.frasercoastholidays.info).

GOLD COAST (177 F2) (⟨ J5⟩

Just 60km (37mi) south of Brisbane is the Gold Coast, a 70km (43½mi)-long stretch of coastline with 35 beaches for surfers, some of which are first class. *Surfers Paradise* is the main centre on the Gold Coast, but its appearance takes some getting used to – a skyline of high-rises that looks more like a major American city. There are several excellent leisure parks in the vicinity that can be seen in the distance from the 300m (984ft)-high Q1 apartment building in Surfers Paradise (Hamilton Avenue) *(Sun–Thu 8am–8.30pm, Fri/Sat 8am–midnight | approx. A$20 | www.q1.com.au)*. For further information see *www.goldcoasttourism.com.au*.

INSIDER TIP ▶ LAMINGTON NATIONAL PARK (177 F2) (⟨ F5⟩

This national park lies inland from the Gold Coast, 180km (112mi) south of Brisbane. A network of paths covering 160km (100mi) runs through the hilly countryside of the McPherson Range. *O'Reilly's Rainforest Guesthouse (25 rooms | Lamington National Park Rd. via Canungra | tel. 07 55 44 06 44 | www.oreillys.com.au | Expensive)* organised excellent guided hikes through the rainforest. Alternative accommodation can be found in the *Binna Burra Mountain Lodge (30 cabins | Beechmont | tel. 07 55 33 37 58 | www.binnaburra lodge.com.au | Moderate–Expensive)*.

SUNSHINE COAST (169 F6) (⟨ J5⟩

Dream-like beaches like the 150km (93mi) stretch between Bribie Island and Fraser Island and pretty resorts. The trip from *Caloundra* to *Noosa Heads* in the north is well worthwhile. This lovely spot *(www. noosaguide.com)*, together with its twin

town *Noosaville*, is the touristic heart of the Sunshine Coast *(www.sunshinecoast. com, www.sunshinecoast.com.au)*.

During the day, people are attracted by wonderfully wide sheltered beaches such as *Main Beach, Marcus Beach* or *Peregian Beach*. Evenings can be spent in one of the many street cafés and restaurants on Hastings St., later you can promenade up and down the boardwalk under a starry sky. You can go for a short walk in the small *Noosa National Park* close by that covers an area of just 1½mi². The rugged sandstone cliff landscape in *Cooloola National Park* to the north can only be explored in a 4×4 *(www.fourwheeldrive. com.au)*. Good places to spend the night can be found under *www.accomnoosa. com.au* and cheap transport links from Brisbane: *tel. 07 54 50 59 33 | www.air shuttle.com.au*

CAIRNS

(161 F5) (⟨ H2⟩ The boomtown of the north (population 140,000) is the perfect starting point for boat trips to the Great Barrier Reef, hikes through the tropical rainforest and adventurous excursions to the northern-most point of Cape York.

CITY ▶ **WHERE TO START?**
The esplanade in the centre is bursting with life: all sorts of eateries, hotels, the lagoon for an inviting swim and streets of shops around the corner. The harbour with boat tours to the Great Barrier Reef is just a short walk away. From the railway station it's about 15 mins. on foot; from the airport just a 10 min. drive by taxi or shuttle bus.

CAIRNS

Before where Bruce Highway ends in the north at Cairns, it passes motels, hotels and blocks of flats that testify to the booming tourist industry. The streets laid out like a chequerboard in the centre are a shopper's paradise, brimming with mass-produced souvenirs, watersports equipment and clothes. As soon as it gets dark, the numerous restaurants and pubs on the esplanade turn on their brightly-coloured neon signs.

See the rainforest from above in the Skyrail cablecar

FLECKER BOTANIC GARDENS

The more than 100 different species of palm tree, orchids and climbers will give you a first impression of the variety of tropical plants. The *Aboriginal Plant Use Garden* contains plants that the Aborigines grew thousands of years ago for food or medicine. *Collins Avenue | Mon–Fri 7.30am–5.30pm, Sat/Sun 8.30am–5.30pm*

SKYRAIL ★

The 7.5km (4½mi)-long cablecar takes you into the mountainous countryside with its fascinating vegetation inland from Cairns. The cabins glide over the valleys and provide views of the waterfalls on *Barron River* too. Explanations on the flora and fauna of the rainforest can be found at two stopping points en route where you can break your trip as you like. The destination is *Kuranda*, once an alternative lifestyle hippie settlement, now a teeming souvenir market. The best way to return is on the *Kuranda Scenic Train* that makes an adventurous and twisty descent back down to the plain. Tip: book the *Ultimate Kuranda Experience*, a day's excursion that starts in the morning at the Tjapukai Cultural Centre, followed by the Skyrail (www.skyrail.com.au) to Kuranda, returning to Cairns in the afternoon on the last train (www.railaustralia.com.au) (approx. A$140, reservations e.g. through *Tourism Tropical North Queensland (see Information p. 80)*.

TJAPUKAI CULTURAL CENTRE ★

The *Aboriginal Cultural Park* is run by the local group of Aborigines and is located next to the *Skyrail* cablecar base station. A tour through the park includes an introduction to the native inhabitants' world of myths and a good film on the history of the Aborigines since the arrival of the

Gain some fascinating insights into how the Aborigines live at the Tjapukai Cultural Centre

white settlers, a visit to a museum, a dance show, a demonstration of the didgeridoo and how to throw a spear and a boomerang. *Reservations, tel. 07 40 42 99 00 | www.tjapukai.com.au*

FOOD & DRINK

OCHRE RESTAURANT ●
Aborigine recipes and ingredients are the attraction of this unusual restaurant. *43 Shields St. | tel. 07 40 51 01 00 | www. ochrerestaurant.com.au | open every day | Moderate*

SHOPPING

At weekends, artists and craftspeople sell their wares on the pier.

SPORTS & ACTIVITIES

ESPLANADE SWIMMING LAGOON ●
Just a few yards from the town centre you can cool off in this well cared-for bathing area with a view of the ocean. What more could you want – especially at it's all free! Tip: bag a barbecue on the lawn for an evening party.

FLYING ADVENTURE
A great experience! Fly with a former coast patrol pilot 300km (185mi) over the Barrier Reef and enjoy the phenomenal view through the specially curved windows *(through Reefwatch Air Tours | tel. 07 40 35 98 08 | www.reefwatch.com | from A$200)*.

EXCURSIONS AND CRUISES TO THE REEF
Day-trips are organised from Cairns to the Outer Reef *(e.g. Sunlover Cruises | tel. 07 40 31 10 55 | www.sunlover.com.au)* as well as visits to small, coral Green Island *(Great Adventures | tel. 07 40 51 56 44 | www.great adventures.com.au)*. Comfortable mini cruises of between 3 and 7 days are run by *Captain Cook Cruises (A$1200–2800 | tel. 07 40 31 44 33 | www.captaincook.com.au)*.

DIVING
Diversionoz in *Palm Cove (20 min. north | tel. 07 40 39 02 00 | www.diversionoz.com)* organises trips lasting one or several days in fast boats to the reef – with diving instruction from A$275.

BAY VILLAGE TROPICAL RETREAT
This small hotel in the middle of Cairns has a garden with tropical plants and a swimming pool. The air-conditioned, tastefully decorated rooms (also for self-caterers) have bamboo furniture. *62 rooms | Lake St./Gatton St. | tel. 07 40 51 46 22 | www.bayvillage.com.au | Moderate–Expensive*

HOLIDAY INN
This pleasant, standard-category hotel is on the edge of the esplanade and therefore central; many of the rooms have a lovely view of the ocean. *237 rooms | tel. 07 40 50 60 70 | www.ichotelsgroup.com | Moderate–Expensive*

INFORMATION

TOURISM TROPICAL NORTH QUEENSLAND
51 The Esplanade | tel. 07 40 51 35 88 | www.cairnsgreatbarrierreef.org.au | www.destinationqueensland.com | www.tropical-australia.de

WHERE TO GO

ATHERTON TABLELAND
(161 E–F5) (*m H2*)
Mountains of volcanic origin covered with dense vegetation tower up 900m (almost 3000ft) 50km (31mi) west of Cairns. Fascinating ecological niches have evolved in ancient craters, around deep lakes and spectacular waterfalls, and are home to a host of tropical birds and rare

animals. One of the loveliest spots is the enigmatic *Mount Hypipamee*, the geological origins of which have still not been explained to this day. There are wonderful waterfalls with crystal-clear waterholes everywhere in the tableland. Four of the most beautiful can be reached on the 15km (9½mi) *Waterfall Circuit* from *Millaa Millaa*. Don't forget your swim things!

The little historical town *Yungaburra* (pop. 1000), that is largely a conservation area, is a good place to stay, e.g. at *Kookaburra Lodge (Eacham Ra./Oak St. | 12 rooms | tel. 07 40 95 32 22 | www.kookaburra-lodge.com | Moderate)*, a small hotel with a garden and pool. There are several good restaurants in Yungaburra *(Nick's Swiss-Italian Restaurant | 33 Gillies Highway | tel. 07 40 95 33 30 | Moderate)* and antique shops. An authentic market is held every 4th Sun in the month in the village *(www.athertontableland.com)*.

INSIDER TIP CAPE YORK
(161 D1) (*m G1*)
Cape York is a destination for those with a real thirst for adventure. The northern-most point in Australia, enclosed on three sides by the sea, is larger than England but this wilderness is home to only about 10,000 people, most of whom are Aborigines living in their own territorial areas or settlements. Large areas of Cape York remain unexplored. Savannas with termite hills several metres high, light-filled eucalyptus forests and rainforest with prolific vegetation. One solitary road leads from Cairns to the end of the continent, known as *The Tip* or *Pajinka*. The 974km (605mi)-long stretch is largely a dust track and only motorable in the dry season between May and October. Petrol and simple places to stay can be found in roadhouses or stations along the route. You should plan 5–6 days for one stretch. All sorts of tour operators offer guided trips from Cairns (e.g. *www.*

wilderness-challenge.com.au, 7 days with a return flight to Cairns, approx. A$2000 per person).

Heritage Site. Ancient giant trees, lianas, ferns, palms and moss give way to a sea of mangrove forests. One of the world's

A hike through the Mossman Gorge takes you across this suspension bridge

DAINTREE NATIONAL PARK AND CAPE TRIBULATION ⭐ (161 F4) (*M H2*)

The protests of committed environmentalists have resulted in Australia's most important and beautiful tropical rainforest being saved from the axe. Today, the breath-taking Daintree National Park, 110km (68mi) north of Cairns, is a protected area and part of a Unesco World largest birds, the flightless *cassowary*, lives in this fantastic wilderness. Saltwater crocodiles can be seen in the two largest rivers in the national park. Boat trips on *Daintree River*, hikes in *Mossmann Gorge* and at dream-like *Cape Tribulation* give a good impression of the fragile beauty of this tropical landscape. Daintree of is great spiritual significance to the local

Kuku Yalanji Aborigines. Along the **INSIDER TIP** *Bama Way* between Daintree River and Cooktown that was opened in 2007, Aboriginal tribes in the region let you gain an insight into their everyday life. You can either book a 2-day tour *(approx. A$300 | tel. 07 40 53 70 01 | www. adventurenorthaustralia.com)* or piece together your own personal tour *(www. bamaway.com.au)*. The road is surfaced as far as Cape Tribulation (a worthwhile destination for a day tour from Cairns or Port Douglas). However, it is narrow in places and leads through the middle of the rainforest. All sorts of places en route invite you to take a break.

MISSION BEACH (161 F5) (*ɱ H2*)
As beach holidays north of Cairns have become very expensive, places such as Mission Beach *(www.missionbeachtourism. com)*, 140km (87mi) to the south are popular, especially among the younger crowd. Mission Beach is a good place to start a hiking *(www.epa.qld.gov.au/parks)* or diving tour *(www.calypsodive.com)*. Day-trips to *Dunk Island* are also possible. Covered in rainforest. it also has a very beautiful resort *(www.dunk-island.com)*. In early 2011, a tropical storm caused considerable damage in the area.

PORT DOUGLAS
(161 F5) (*ɱ H2*)
The *Captain Cook Highway* is a superb panoramic route running along the coast to Port Douglas (pop. 5000), 70km (43½mi) north of Cairns. Until the end of the 1980s, this was a modest little village that has now been transformed into a sophisticated holiday resort with generally excellent hotels and restaurants which charge correspondingly high prices *(www.portdouglaswebs.com.au)*.
Four Mile Beach is an immaculate stretch of beach that starts at the end of *Macrossan Street*, the main road of shops. Every morning, at least a dozen sailing boats and catamarans set off for the Great Barrier Reef. Boats operated by *Quicksilver* moor about 90 mins. later at a pontoon on the Outer Reef protected from the waves, from where diving and snorkelling tours start *(tel. 07 40 87 21 00 | www. quicksilver-cruises.com)*.

PALM COVE (161 F5) (*ɱ H2*)
Of all the various sections of beach north of Cairns, Palm Cove (approx. 20 mins. drive) is among the most glamorous. Luxury resort hotels, cafés and restaurants line the 1.5km (1mi)-long promenade next to the pristine palm beach. *Peppers Beach House (169 rooms | 123 Williams Esplanade | tel. 07 40 59 92 00 | www.peppers.com.au | Expensive)*, with lovely spacious grounds and a pool area surrounded by sand, is at the very centre. The (manned) beach is opposite.

TOWNSVILLE

(168 C1) (*ɱ H3*) This busy harbour town (pop. 105,000) with its magnificent colonial buildings, 280km (174mi) south of Cairns, is the economic hub of the tropical north.
The attractively laid out promenade, The Strand, with lots of restaurants, swimming pools and beaches (with stingray nets) is the perfect place to relax.

SIGHTSEEING

REEF HQ
The fascinating display of the undersea world around the *Great Barrier Reef,* shown here in a huge aquarium, should not be missed. *Daily 9.30am–5pm | 2 Flinders Street East | www.reefhq.com.au and www. gbrmpa.gov.au | A$28;* the *Imax Theatre*

Townsville with its harbour is the economic hub of the tropical north

with a huge screen and the *Museum of Tropical Queensland* with a dinosaur exhibition are in the building next door.

FOOD & DRINK

THE WATERMARK
Café and restaurant in trendy, cool design with modern Australian cuisine. The terrace has a view to the park and sea on the other side of the road. *72 The Strand | tel. 07 4772 3133 | open every day | Expensive*

WHERE TO STAY

STRAND PARK HOTEL
Some of the 45 suites in this spacious holiday flat complex have a view of *Magnetic Island*. The beach is right in front and the centre of Townsville just a short stroll away. *59–60 The Strand | tel. 07 4750 78 88 | www.strandparkhotel.com.au | Moderate*

INFORMATION

VISITOR INFORMATION
Flinders Mall | tel. 07 4721 36 60 | www.townsvilleonline.com.au www.townsvilleholidays.info

WHERE TO GO

MAGNETIC ISLAND
(168 C1) *(𝄞 H3)*
This holiday island with its rather average beaches, lies 8km (5mi/approx. 20 mins.) from Townsville and is popular among day-trippers. Ferries *(approx. A\$33 return)* run several times a day from Breakwater Terminal *(Sealink | Sir Leslie Thiess Drive | tel. 07 4771 38 55 | www.sealinkqld.com.au).*

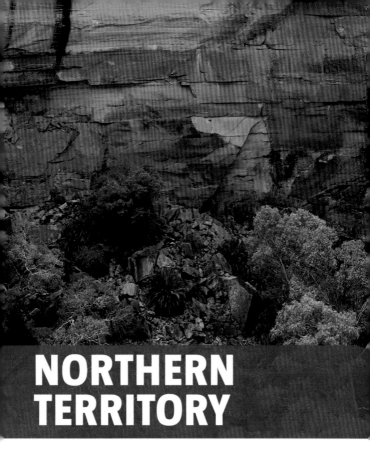

NORTHERN TERRITORY

From the tropical north to the red deserts in the heart of the country, this remote and sparsely populated region of Australia offers starkly contrasting scenery and a wide variety of tourist attractions.

In 1863, Northern Territory (pop. 230,000) was part of Southern Australia with Palmerston – later renamed Darwin – as its capital. A gold rush led to a flood of newcomers in 1874. Darwin has been virtually wiped off the map twice: in 1940 by bombing by the Japanese and in 1974 by Cyclone Tracy. But despite this, Northern Territory has developed into an important destination for millions of visitors. Today, 'the Territory' – which covers 520,000mi² – is a producer of raw materials, beef, pearls, crocodile meat and fish.

ALICE SPRINGS

(166 A4) (🗺 E4) **The red centre of the country with Alice Springs (pop. 28,000) as its heart, is one of the most important magnets for tourists.**

Uluru – as the Anangu Aborigines call Ayers Rock – has become a symbol for the red continent as a whole over the past 20 or so years. But it is not only this im-

Endless wilderness: lonely deserts, hidden waterfalls and a wild coastline where crocodiles bask in the sun

posing monolith that you simply have to have seen. The MacDonnell Ranges and Kings Canyon are just as impressive.

SIGHTSEEING

INSIDER TIP ALICE SPRINGS DESERT PARK

The park is a mixture of museum and zoological garden and gives a good idea of the natural history of the surrounding desert. *Larapinta Drive | daily 7.30am–6pm | A\$20*

ANZAC HILL ☀

From here you have a good view over Alice Springs and over the whole of the surrounding area. The MacDonnell Ranges turn a wonderful red especially at sunrise and sunset.

OLD TELEGRAPH STATION RESERVE
This lovingly renovated telegraph station, built of hewn rock in 1872, takes you back to Australia's pioneering days. *North Stuart Highway | daily winter 8am–7pm, summer 8am–9pm | A$5*

ROYAL FLYING DOCTOR SERVICE
In 1939, a flying doctor service opened its offices in Alice Springs. The 15-minute video that provides a very interesting insight into the work of the RFDS is shown every in. *80 Head Street | www.assoa.nt.edu.au | Mon–Sat 8.30am–4.30pm, Sun 1.30pm–4.30pm | A$8*

SHOPPING

INSIDER TIP Aboriginal art in the typical dot style from the desert community of Papunya, 240km (150mi) northwest, is not only a beautiful souvenir, but – depending on the artist – can also be an investment. Direct sales of works from

Aborigine art in Papunya Tula Gallery in Alice Springs

half an hour. After that you can listen in to the radio communications for a few minutes and look at the memorabilia. *8–10 Stuart Terrace | Mon–Sat 9am–4pm, Sun 1pm–4pm | A$9*

SCHOOL OF THE AIR
There's a lot of space in the world's largest classroom: 520,000mi². Children in the outback get their lessons from hundred's of miles away now in their own living rooms via the Internet. You can watch the teacher through a glass window and listen

Papunya can be found at *Papunya Tula Artists | 63 Todd Mall | www.papunyatula. com.au.* Ask for a certificate of authenticity for more expensive works! For more information see: *www.ankaaa.org.au* and *www.desart.com.au*

ENTERTAINMENT

Fancy a rustic INSIDER TIP outback pub crawl? *Bojangles Saloon & Restaurant, 80 Todd Street,* (live broadcasts of concerts and the pub atmosphere can be called up on the Internet under *www.bossaloon. com.au*) is a good place for a drink, as is *Todd Tavern (1 Todd Mall)*. But a word of warning: in the past, there have been repeated confrontations between drunken Aborigines and unsuspecting tourists.

WHERE TO STAY

CROWNE PLAZA

A popular 4½-star hotel slightly away from the town centre. Excellent Thai restauant *Hanuman (www.hanuman.com. au)*. *178 rooms | 82 Barret Drive | tel. 08 89 50 80 00 | www.ichtelsgroup.com | Moderate*

DIPLOMAT ALICE SPRINGS

Plum in the middle of the town, with the very good restaurant *Kellers* right next door. *58 rooms | Hartley Street/Gregory Terrace | tel. 08 89 52 89 77 | www.diplomat motel.com.au | Moderate*

INFORMATION

CENTRAL AUSTRALIAN TOURISM INDUSTRY ASSOCIATION

Gregory Terrace/Todd Mall | tel. 08 89 52 58 00 | www.travelnt.com | www.central australiantourism.com

WHERE TO GO

HERMANNSBURG (165 F4) (*𝄞 E4*)
This village (pop. 450), inhabited largely by Aborigines, 126km (78mi) west of Alice Springs, has a former Lutheran missionary station. A good and slightly disturbing exhibition is a reminder of the not always successful attempt to convert the indigenous people to Christianity by trying to implement the typically German values of 'order and discipline'.
Well-known residents of Hermannsburg include the Aboriginal painter Albert Namatjira (1902–59), the founder of a new, more western-orientated style of outback painting, and Professor Ted Strehlow (1908–78), a leading ethnologist who researched into the culture of the Arrente Aborigines in central Australia. *Missionary station March–Nov daily, Dec–Feb Wed–Mon 9am–5pm | A$7*

KINGS CANYON (WATARRKA) ★
(165 E4) (*𝄞 E4*)
Until just a few years ago, Kings Canyon – 420km (260mi) southwest of Alice Springs – was an insider tip for backpackers. It has since developed into one of the major attractions in Northern Territory. Tarmaced roads now lead from Alice Springs and Uluru along *Lasseter Highway* and *Luritja Road*, almost as far as the entrance to this sandstone canyon millions of years old, with rock walls rising up to 270m (886ft). Alternatively, take

---

★ **Kings Canyon (Watarrka)**
Once an insider tip, now a magnet for thousands of tourists: hiking through a rocky landscape millions of years old → p. 87

★ **Uluru and Kata Tjuta**
A red monolith and 36 mysterious 'heads' → p. 88

★ **Kakadu National Park**
Impressive wilderness in the tropical north of the Territory and one of the best-known nature reserves in Australia → p. 93

★ **Katherine Gorge**
One of the most beautiful gorges anywhere in the country → p. 95

MARCO POLO HIGHLIGHTS

the route via the *Mereenie Loop* from Glen Helen or Hermannsburg which should only be tackled in a 4×4. Two hikes of differing degrees of difficulty are offered in Kings Canyon.

Accommodation can be found 7km (4½mi) before reaching the canyon in *Kings Canyon Resort (tel. 08 89 56 74 42 | www.kingscan*

Alice Springs and can be reached in a normal car along a tarmaced road. Unlike any other natural wonder, this 348m (1142ft)-high monolith that, rather like an iceberg, reaches miles down into the ground below it, has evolved into a symbol for Australia. Uluru attracts hundreds of thousands of visitors every year to the

The Kata Tjuta comprise 36 rounded rocks

yonresort.com.au | Moderate–Expensive) or *Kings Creek Station (tel. 08 89 56 74 74 | www.kingscreekstation.com.au | Budget)*, a farm that is however 35km (22mi) from the canyon. Hikes through Kings Canyon should only be tackled in the cool of the day. Take plenty of water!

ULURU & KATA TJUTA ★ ●
(165 E5) (*ɯ E4*)

Uluru, or *Ayers Rock*, as it used to be called, is some 450km (280mi) southwest of

red heart of the continent. For Anangu Aborigines, however, it is the site with the greatest spiritual meaning and an important testimony to their Story of Creation. The rock was named by the explorer William Gosse in 1873. Since 1985, Uluru and 'neighbouring' Kata Tjuta ('The Olgas') have been made into a national park covering 512mi² and have been returned to the Anangu.

The entrance to the park is about 15km (9mi) from Uluru. There are two carparks along this stretch from which the sunrise or sunset can be watched – and it is worth getting there in good time. Please note: alcohol is forbidden. Organised tour groups are however exempted. There are also several carparks at Uluru itself from which you can explore the base of the rock. For some time now, the Aborigines have been demanding that climbing their sacred site be prohibited. A much better alternative to a climb is the 9.4km (5¾mi) route around the monolith. *Anangu Tours* (*www.ananguwaai.com.au*), operated by Aborigines themselves, offers very good tours. On the *Liru Walk*, for example, the traditional owners of Uluru explain the mythology connected with the rock and show how they have survived for thousands of years in an area that for Europeans is seemingly barren. Hikes can be booked in the resort and in the *Uluru-Kata Tjuta Cultural Centre* in the park. This centre also houses an interesting exhibition on the culture of the Anangu and the natural history of the park, and is a perfect starting point for a visit to Uluru.

50km (31mi) from Uluru is Kata Tjuta ('Many Heads'), a collection of 36 rounded, domed rocks covering 13½mi². The highest is almost 200m (656ft) higher than Uluru. Many people find 'the Olgas' – as these rock formations used to be called – more attractive than the much better-known Uluru. You can go for lovely walks through the rocks and marvel at the rich, orange-red colours of the central Australian desert. A hike through the *Valley of the Winds* takes around 3 hours and can be particularly recommended. The temperature however can really be a torture; always take enough water with you. In cooler weather, an icy wind blows through the gorge; in summer, the high temperatures turn the area into one huge oven. Hikes should always be planned for the cooler hours of the day.

Ayers Rock Resort (Yulara) caters for everything one might need at Uluru and is approx. 15km (9mi) from the rock and 6km (4mi) from the airport. There is a popular pizza restaurant and snack bar, a supermarket, a booking office and souvenir and clothes shops. Hotels of all standards (incl. a campsite) have been established here but, as there are no alternatives, they are very expensive (*information under: www.ayersrockresort.com.au*). One highlight is the *Sounds of Silence Dinner*: at sunset, beautifully set tables are put up in the desert some distance from Uluru and a buffet served. The evening around the campfire finishes with star gazing (*www.ayersrockresort.com.au/sounds-of-silence*, approx. A$165 per person.).

DARWIN

(158 B2) (*ᗰ D1*) **The capital city of the Northern Territory is the point of arrival or departure for most guests to the region and for visitors to the world-famous Kakadu National Park.**

WHERE TO START?
At the lower end of **Mitchell Street** you'll find yourself in the thick of things. Highway 1 leads into and out of the city. A car is useful if you want to visit the attractive markets in the north or a restaurant in Cullen Bay in the evening. Parking in the centre is no problem. If you're travelling by train (Ghan), the station is unfortunately 15km (9½mi) from the city centre (Berrimah Road) and you have to take a shuttle bus or taxi. It is some 12km (7½mi) from the airport.

Darwin (population 120,000) today is a mixture of a modern international metropolis and a provincial town. Surrounded by the Arafura Sea, the capital is in a particularly attractive setting. The weather, however, is not to everyone's taste: it's either hot and bone dry (May–October) or hot and sticky. Thanks to its proximity to Asia and the flood of immigrants, the high proportion of Aborigines and Europeans, Darwin has the INSIDER TIP greatest ethnic diversity of any city in Australia.

SIGHTSEEING

AQUASCENE FISH FEEDING
Every day at high tide, fish come close to the shoreline at Doctor's Gully to be fed (www.aquascene.com.au). Not necessarily everyone's cup of tea, but fun for the children.

BOTANIC GARDEN
In 1870, the gardener Maurice Holtz laid out Darwin's magnificent botanic park. Although Cyclone Tracy decimated 80% of the plants and trees in 1974, it has recovered surprisingly quickly. With more than 400 species of palm tree that partly grow in a miniature rainforest, a small orchid nursery and an artificial waterfall and swamp, the garden – that covers 104 acres – is one of the botanic gardens with the greatest variety of species in the southern hemisphere. *Gilruth Avenue/Gardens Road | daily 7am–8pm | admission free*

CROCODYLUS PARK
The professionally run park is a safe introduction to these huge reptiles. *815 McMillans Road (Knuckey Lagoon)*, approx. 15 min. drive from Darwin City towards the airport, *daily 9am–5pm, tours and feeding lasting 1 hour: 10am, noon, 2pm and 3.30pm, A$30, www.crocodylus park.com*

FANNY BAY GAOL MUSEUM
The old prison is a showcase for the area's criminal past. For almost 100 years, up until 1979, offenders were locked up here. Visitors can explore the site free of charge. The gallows can also to be seen where the last execution in Northern Territory was carried out in 1952. *East Point Road | daily 10am–4pm*

MUSEUM & ART GALLERY OF THE NORTHERN TERRITORY
The museum provides a very good insight into the culture and natural history of Northern Territory. There is an interesting collection of Aborigine art. The display on Cyclone Tracy is also well worth seeing. The *Darwin Ski Club* opposite has an excellent beer garden. *Conacher Street Fannie Bay | Mon–Sat 9am–5pm, Sun 10am–5pm | admission free*

FOOD & DRINK

The revamping of Wharf Precinct, to include the addition of a large convention centre, will take until 2015. Until it's finished, the many restaurants on *Stokes Hill Wharf* will whet your appetite. They can be reached quickly by taking the lift at the end of Smith Street at the Vibe and Medina hotels and the swimming lagoon. The selection of restaurants along *Mitchell Street* and at the *Cullen Bay Marina* is also big.

PEE WEE'S
Under palm trees with a great view of Fanny Bay, here you can indulge in creative Australian food and good wines. *Alec Fong Lim Drive East Point Reserve | tel. 08 89 81 68 68 | open every day | Expensive*

SHOPPING

Darwin is well known for its many markets, e.g. the *Parap Market* on Sat mornings and the *Mindil Beach Sunset Market (Gilruth Avenue/Fannie Bay | April–Oct Thu and Sun 5pm–10pm or 4pm–9pm)* as well as the *Rapid Creek Market (Rapid Creek Business Village | 48 Trower Road, approx. 10 mins. from Darwin City | Fri 3pm–9pm, Sun 6.30am–1pm)*. For more information on all markets (and in other cities) see: *www.marketsonline.com.au.* Territory's culture pearls can be marvelled at the INSIDER TIP *Australian Pearling Exhibition (Kitchener Drive | Stokes Hill Wharf | daily 10am–3pm | approx. A$7)* and are available from *Paspaley Pearls (Bennett Street/Smith Street Mall)*. The best address for freshly caught fish is *Frances Bay*. At *Mr. Barra* behind Fishermans Wharf and in *Darwin Fish Market (Shed 5)*, the displays full of all sorts of seafood and shellfish make your mouth

water (access via *Frances Bay Drive)*. *Framed (55 Stuart Highway | www.framed. com.au)* and *Mason Gallery (7/21 Cavenagh Street | www.masongallery.com.au)* are among the best art galleries. *Readback Book Exchange* sells good (certified) Aborigine art at lower prices *(32 Smith Street Mall)*. Note: if shipping to Europe, works of art are subject to tax based on their value!

SPORTS & ACTIVITIES

EAST POINT RESERVE
The park on the beach close to the city centre is a popular place for picnics and relaxing and for swimming in Lake Alexander – a saltwater basin that is free of dangerous stinger jellyfish all year round.

Well visited: the restaurants on Wharf Precinct in Darwin

A night in the tropics: the open-air Deckchair Cinema in Darwin

ENTERTAINMENT

INSIDER TIP DECKCHAIR CINEMA

The open-air cinema, run by the Darwin Film Society and open between April and Nov, has 250 deckchairs and 100 seats. Cushions can be hired. Don't forget to bring a mosquito net! Food and drink are available (beer and wine after 6.30pm). The atmosphere near Darwin harbour is unique. Films start at around 7.30pm; a second showing – usually at weekends – begins around 9.30pm *(www.deckchair cinema.com.au). Entrance on the esplanade or Jervois Road on Wharf Precinct*

SUNSET CRUISE

With such wonderful sunsets, an atmospheric boat-trip in the late afternoon around the extensive harbour bay is a good idea. Perhaps combine it with a delicious dinner on board the nostalgic schooner 'Alfred Nobel'. This is topped off by good wine and a refreshing breeze; the wonderful views of the tropical coastline complement this perfect picture. *Darwin Harbour Cruises | from Stokes Wharf | daily 5.45pm–8.30pm | tel. 08 89 42 31 31 | www.darwin harbourcruises.com.au*

WHERE TO STAY

CAMPING

The well-equipped *Hidden Valley Tourist Park (25 Hidden Valley Road | tel. 08 89 84 28 88 | www.hiddenvalleytouristpark.com. au | Budget)* is conveniently situated on Stuart Highway, not far from the airport. The extensive *Lee Point Village Resort (Lee Point Road | tel. 08 89 45 05 35 | www. leepointvillageresort.com.au | Budget)* is north of the city close to the sea at far-flung and lonely Lee Point. Both sites also have cabins.

CULLEN BAY SERVICED FLATS

Modern apartment hotel with cooking facilities. *95 rooms | 26 Marine Boulevard | tel. 08 89 81 79 99 | www.cullenbayapts. com.au | Moderate–Expensive*

MANTRA ON THE ESPLANADE

The lovely superior hotel is close to Darwin Harbour. *204 rooms | 88 The Esplanade | tel. 08 89 43 43 33 | www. mantra.com.au | Moderate–Expensive*

INFORMATION

TOURISM TOP END VISITOR CENTRE
Smith Street/Knuckey Street (at the end of the Mall) | tel. 08 89 80 60 00 | www. tourismtopend.com.au | www.travelnt. com | www.tourismnt.com.au

WHERE TO GO

LITCHFIELD NATIONAL PARK
(158 B2) (*ɷ D1*)

This national park, some 160km (100mi) south of Darwin, is a wild oasis with water-falls, gorges, rainforest and huge termite hills. You can swim in a number of water-holes without having to worry about crocodiles. The *Wangi Falls* and *Florence Falls* are particularly beautiful and very popular – and are great for swimming. There are several simple campsites in the vicinity.

TERRITORY WILDLIFE PARK
(158 B2) (*ɷ D1*)

Large, partly renaturalised park that pro-vides a very good insight into the fauna and flora of Northern Territory. *Berry Springs | 60km (37mi) south of Darwin | daily 8.30am–6pm | A$20 | www.territo-rywildlifepark.com.au*

TIWI ISLANDS (158 B–C1) (*ɷ D–E1*)

Some 80km (50mi) off the coast are the two islands *Melville* and *Bathurst,* inhab-ited by Aborigines who have developed their very own culture here and are well known for their craftwork and painting. Tourism is carefully regulated. Those want-ing to visit the islands can only do so as part of a guided tour. The one-day excur-sion by air shows you a great deal of Bathurst Island, the main island, and enables visitors to meet the indigenous people and learn about their traditions *(Tiwi Tours | March–Nov Mon–Fri from Darwin Airport | 7am–5.15pm | tel. 08 89 23 65 23 or 1300 72 13 65 | www.aus-sieadventure.com.au | A$470 per person).* A ship also travels regularly to the islands.

KAKADU NATIONAL PARK

(158–159 C–D2) (*ɷ E1*) ★ **One of the best-known national parks in Australia, it is 255km (158mi) east of Darwin in the western part of the Arnhem Land Escarpment, that runs 500km (310mi) from north to south, separting it from the scarcely populated region of Arnhem Land in the east.**

LOW BUDGET

▶ Eat fresh oysters at sunset on Mindil Beach. This delicacy can be bought on the spot for just a few dol-lars at the *Mindil Beach Sunset Market (Fanny Bay, April–Oct)* held on Thu and Sun.

▶ When it is not too hot, it's not as mad as it may sound – explore Alice Springs by bike. If there are no bikes for hire where you are staying, have one brought to you from *Alice Bike Hire (tel. 04 39 86 07 35 | www. longhorn.net.au | from A$30).*

Due to its natural and cultural importance, the national park has been added to the Unesco list of World Heritage Sites. It can be reached along the surfaced Arnhem Highway in a conventional car. The main centre of the park that covers 7300mi², is *Jabiru*, where you can find places to stay to suit every wallet, as well as provisions. You should plan at least 2–3 days for a visit to the park. The pass costs A$25 per vehicle *(available from the Bowali Visitor Centre)*.

SIGHTSEEING

A visit to *Yellow Waters Creek* is quite an experience. On a boat-trip through the wetlands you will see not only the dangerous saltwater crocodile but some 280 species of bird and 1600 plant species. The best time for the 2-hour boat-trip is in the early evening during the dry season (June–Oct). Tours start at *Gagudju Lodge* in *Cooinda (Yellow Water Cruises | tel. 08 89 79 01 45 | www.yellowwatercruises.com)*. It is just a few yards from the generously laid-out *Gagudju Lodge Cooinda*, with its campsite and restaurants, to the jetty where the boats leave *(48 rooms and pitches| signposted on the Kakadu Highway | tel. 08 89 79 01 45 | www.gagudjulodgecooinda.com.au | Budget–Expensive)*.

The *Jim Jim Falls* and *Twin Falls*, two spectacular waterfalls, are equally well worth seeing. The 70km (44mi) between the Kakadu Highway and the two natural sights can, however, only be covered in a 4×4. One highlight is 1.5km (1mi)-long circular walk to the rock paintings at *Nourlangie Rock*, especially the picture of a figure in the aboriginal x-ray style, that are thousands of years old. The rock painting site in *Ubirr*, 40km (25mi) north of Arnhem Highway, is less visited due to its distance from the other tourist attractions.

Please note: although the road is tarmaced, it is often impassable in the rainy season.

WHERE TO STAY

AURORA KAKADU HOTEL
This complex in Jabiru offers a variety of different accommodation (138 rooms and a campsite). *Tel. 08 89 79 24 22 | www.auroraresorts.com.au | Budget–Moderate*

GAGUDJU CROCODILE HOLIDAY INN ●
The best hotel in the whole of the national park. The building is in the shape of a crocodile. *110 rooms | tel. 08 89 79 90 00 | www.ichotelsgroup.com | Expensive*

INFORMATION

BOWALI VISITOR CENTRE
The tourist information centre just outside Jabiru is a must for all visitors to Kakadu National Park: good exhibition on the history of the park, maps and other helpful information. *Tel. 08 89 38 11 21 | www.environment.gov.au | www.kakadunationalparkaustralia.com*

KATHERINE

(158 C3) (ⓜ E2–3) This small town (pop. 10,000) is the first or last stop between Darwin and Alice Springs and the starting point for trips to the border with Western Australia.
Tourism is correspondingly important for Katherine, although many locals work in the neighbouring gold mine or in agriculture. In the past few years, the region has made a name as a destination in its own right thanks to *Katherine Gorge* in Nitmiluk National Park.

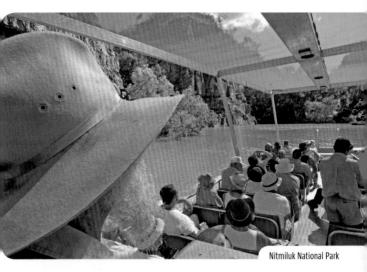

Nitmiluk National Park

WHERE TO STAY

RIVERVIEW TOURIST VILLAGE AND HOT SPRINGS

The big plus point for this well-managed campsite with motel rooms and cabins, approx. 2km (1¼mi) from the town centre, is that it is just a short walk from Katherine Hot Springs – pure bliss for the feet after a strenuous hike. You can also get to know the locals on the banks in the shade of the trees and bushes. *440 Victoria Highway | tel. 08 89 72 10 11 | www.riverviewtouristvillage.com.au | Budget–Moderate*

INFORMATION

KATHERINE VISITOR CENTRE

Lindsay Street/Katherine Terrace | tel. 08 89 72 26 50 | www.visitkatherine.com.au

WHERE TO GO

ARNHEM LAND (158 C3) (*ϕ E2*)

A visit to INSIDER TIP *Arnhem Land*, a largely unexploited nature reserve and one of the last areas untouched by mass tourism, is well worth it. Completely managed by the Yolngu Aborigines, only a small number of visitors are allowed there for cultural reasons. As a result, it has retained its unique atmosphere. For tours and information: *Davidson's Arnhemland Safaris | tel. 08 89 27 52 40 | www.arnhemland-safaris.com.*

NITMILUK NATIONAL PARK

(158 C3) (*ϕ E1*)

The entrance to the park is some 30km (19mi) east of Katherine. This is also where boat-trips through the ★ *Katherine Gorge* start *(www.travelnorth.com.au)*. The gorge is home to numerous animals and plants and of great spiritual importance to the Aborigines.

42km (26mi) north of Katherine on Stuart Highway is the turning to ● INSIDER TIP *Edith Falls* that are also in Nitmiluk National Park. Camping is permitted here – a good place to spend the night for all those who don't want to stay in Katherine itself.

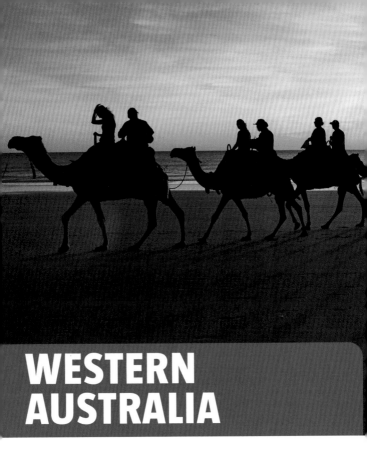

WESTERN AUSTRALIA

Extending over some 1,000,000mi², the state of Western Australia covers around one third of the continent's overall area. However, only 2.4 million people – just one tenth of the total population – live is this part of the country, characterised by the red of the desert and the blue of the Indian Ocean.

The capital, Perth, was founded in 1829. However, it wasn't until 1850 that the new colony really started to develop when convicts were put to work building roads. The 2200km (1370mi)-long Highway 1 from Perth to Broome in the north passes through one of the most interesting and beautiful parts of the country.

Deserted beaches, magnificent geological formations, such as the Pinnacles north of Perth, and endless fields of wild flowers make up the picture of the so-called Outback Coast.

BROOME

(156 C4) (*∅ C2*) **Broome (pop. 14,000) is the unofficial capital of Kimberley. Once an isolated outpost of civilisation, the town has evolved into a tourist destination for Australians looking to escape the winter, thanks to its pleasant climate and the laid-back, tropical lifestyle.**

Photo: Camel ride on Cable Beach

Huge expanses of open country, desert and sea – and hardly any people: Western Australia has something special for everyone

More and more successful professionals from the southern states are choosing to live in Broome. Up until 1910, the town was the world's leading centre of the cultured pearl farming and pearling industry. Today, pearl production only plays a secondary – albeit still important – role. Tourism has become Broome's main industry, due to the superb beaches and as a base to explore the area.

SIGHTSEEING

CABLE BEACH ●

The 22km (14mi)-long sandy beach that starts some 6km (4mi) from the town centre is Broome's biggest attraction *(www.broomecam.com)*. The phenomenon called the INSIDER TIP ▶ *Staircase to the Moon* that can be seen between March and October is a unique natural spectacle.

Broome was once the world's leading pearl farming centre

It occurs three times a month when the full moon shines across the mudflats at Roebuck Bay at low tide. Exact dates can be obtained from the tourist office.

WILDERNESS PARK
Malcolm Douglas, the real 'Crocodile Dundee', made a name for himself catching dangerous saltwater crocodiles. He was killed in a car accident in 2010. In his large park, more than 200 crocodiles and other wild animals can be seen. *Great Northern Highway | some 16km (10mi) from Broome | www.malcolmdouglas.com.au*

FOOD & DRINK

MATSO'S CAFÉ & BREWERY
A legend in Broome. Restaurant with own brewery. *60 Hammersly Street | tel. 08 91 93 58 11 | www.matsos.com.au | open every day | Moderate*

TIDES BAR AND GARDEN RESTAURANT ☆
Lovely terrace with a view over Roebuck Bay, known for its BBQ specialites. *47 Carnavon Street | Mangrove Resort | tel. 08 91 92 13 03 | www.mangrovehotel.com. au | open every day | Moderate*

SHOPPING

Several shops in the centre sell pearls. The cheapest freshwater pearls are not from here but are imported from Asia.

WHERE TO STAY

BROOME BEACH RESORT
New resort with pleasantly furnished cabins of various sizes near Cable Beach. *4 Murray Road | tel. 08 91 58 33 00 | www. broomebeachresort.com | Moderate– Expensive*

BBO CAMPGROUND

An ideal campsite for bird and nature-lovers on Roebuck Bay (no electrcial hook-ups; several cabins for rent), approx. 25km (15½mi) from Broome. This bird observatory is considered by ornithologists to be one of the five most important in the world. *Crab Creek Road | 6km (3¾mi) unsurfaced road | tel. 08 9193 56 00 | www.broomebirdobservatory.com | Budget*

CABLE BEACH CLUB RESORT

The top address in Broome, right on Cable Beach. The typical architectural style using corrugated iron gives the complex a special character of its own. *Tel. 08 9192 04 00 | www.cablebeachclub.com | Expensive*

INFORMATION

BROOME VISITOR CENTRE

Broome Highway corner Bagot Street | tel. 08 9192 22 22 | www.broomevisitorcentre. com.au

WHERE TO GO

INSIDER TIP CAPE LEVEQUE

(156 C3) (*ɯ C2*)

Wild Dampier Peninsula that largely belongs to the Aborigines, is perfect for off-road driving enthusiasts. A 200km (125mi)-long sand and dust track leads north to Cape Leveque, where you can fish or sunbathe on deserted beaches. *Kooljaman campsite (tel. 08 9192 49 70 | www.kooljaman.com.au | Budget–Expensive)* has luxury safari tents, cabins and pitches for your own tent. Advance booking is essential.

WILLIE CREEK PEARL FARM

(156 C4) (*ɯ C2*)

The pearl station some 40km (29mi) north of Broome is a good introduction to the art of pearl farming. *Bookings, tel. 08 9193 60 00 | www.williecreekpearls.com.au*

EXMOUTH

(162 A2) (*ɯ A4*) **This village (pop. 2000) at the tip of North West Cape has evolved into a starting point for tourists who want to explore one of the last virtually untouched coral reefs in the world.**

The Ningaloo Reef is a prize jewel in Australia's natural treasure trove.

WHERE TO STAY

SEABREEZE RESORT

Child-friendly, standard-category hotel next to the Naval Base; good restaurant. *116 North C Street | tel. 08 99 49 18 00 | www. seabreezeresort.com.au | Moderate*

MARCO POLO HIGHLIGHTS

★ **Ningaloo Reef**
One of the most beautiful and varied coral reefs in the world, home to many sea creatures, stretches down the west coast of Australia
→ p. 100

★ **Kimberley**
Unique wilderness and isolation
→ p. 101

★ **Pinnacles (Nambung) National Park**
Bizarre towering rock needles in the middle of a lonely sandy desert → p. 109

★ **Wave Rock**
Interesting geological formation 350km (217mi) southeast of Perth → p. 109

INFORMATION

EXMOUTH VISITORS CENTRE
Murat Road | tel. 08 99 49 11 76 | www.ex mouthwa.com.au | www.mycoralcoast. com.au

WHERE TO GO

CAPE RANGE NATIONAL PARK
(162 A2) (*∅ A4*)
The national park bordering Ningaloo Reef is 39km (24mi) from Exmouth and is outstanding due to its number of unique geological features, fossils and 630 flowering plants. A tour with INSIDERTIP Ningaloo Safari Tours *(23 Ningaloo Street | tel. 08 99 49 15 50 | www.ningaloo safari.com | A$195)* will give you a good idea of the park's beauty. The exclusive *Wild Bush Luxury Camp Sal Salis* comprises 9 tents on the beach and is perfect for

snorkellers *(www.salsalis.com.au, approx. A$730 per person incl. food and drink)*.

KARIJINI NATIONAL PARK
(162–163 C–D3) (*∅ B4*)
Located 500km (310mi) to the east, Karijini is the second largest national park in the state, covering 2320mi² and, with its orangey-red rock formations, its scenery is considered the most spectacular. Accommodation and provisions in *Tom Price* and *Paraburdoo.* Camping is permitted in the park.

MONKEY MIA
(162 A5) (*∅ A4*)
In Monkey Mia, 40km (25mi) to the south, you can watch dolphins at close quarters. Most mornings the animals swim right next to the beach (A$8 per person) and can be fed – strictly regulated – standing knee-deep in the water *(www.monkey miadolphins.org)*. Tens of thousands of visitors come to this area of Shark Bay as a result. This practice is however not without controversy. Critics believe that feeding makes the animals dependent on humans. *Monkey Mia Dolphin Resort (Monkey Mia Road | Shark Bay | tel. 08 99 48 13 20 | www. monkeymia.com.au | Budget–Expensive)* is a camping and hotel complex with accommodation in various price categories.

NINGALOO REEF ★
(162 A3) (*∅ A4*)
The 260km (162mi)-long reef, designated a marine park in 1987, stretches from the small coastal village of *Coral Bay (www. coralbay.org)* along the peninsula to the north. With regard to its beauty and variety, it is absolutely on a par with the Barrier Reef to the east of Australia. It is home to at least 220 different types of coral and 500 species of fish. The confluence of ocean currents rich in nutrients and its proximity ot the Continental Shelf,

LOW BUDGET

▶ 4 free bus routes are an open invitation to explore Perth: the Red Cat bus travels in an east/west direction, the Blue Cat bus north/ south, the Yellow Cat bus from the Entertainment Centre to East Perth and the Orange Cat bus in Fremantle *(www.transperth.wa.gov.au)*.

▶ For budding ornithologists, the remote *Eyre Bird Observatory*, 50km (31mi) south of Cocklebiddy, is a perfect base. The former telegraph station now provides full board in harmony with the natural environment for approx. A$90 per person. *(tel. 08 90 39 34 50 | www. eyrebirds.org)*.

explain why there are some many different species. Four species of ocean turtle live on the reef, as do manta rays, humpback whales, dugongs and various kinds of shark. Ningaloo Reef has gained a reputation as one of the very few places where whale sharks can be watched from close quarters. Snorkellers can swim with these marine animals that grow to up to 18m (60ft) long – a unique experience. But 'no

KIMBERLEY

(157 D–F 2–4) (*Ⓜ C–D2*) ★ **The Kimberley region in the north is something for the more adventurous. Massive canyons, waterfalls, endless horizons and a unique form of rock painting attract people to the far north of Western Australia.**

Dolphins being fed in the morning in Monkey Mia

worries': these huge beasts are plankton eaters and are not dangerous at all.

Unlike the Barrier Reef, Ningaloo Reef can be reached on foot from the mainland. In lagoons such as *Turquoise Bay* 60km (37mi) south of Exmouth, you can take a look at the variety of coral and fish in waist-deep water equipped with just goggles and a snorkel. Diving tours are organised by tour operators *(e.g. www. ningalooreefdive.com)* to the outer reaches of the reef and snorkelling expeditions to the whale sharks (high season between April and June).

Huge swathes of this nature reserve covering 164,000mi² between the towns of Broome in the west and Kununurra in the east are largely uninhabited. The largely untouched scenery is some of the most beautiful Australia has to offer. A journey through Kimberley not only takes a considerable amount of time, it can also be a real challenge.

Although the Great Northern Highway, that runs 1000km (620mi) from Broome to Kununurra, is passable all year round, detours to the countless canyons can only be made in a 4×4. During the wet season, large areas are completely submerged. The best time to travel is May/June and September/October. In July and August many motels and campsites, even in the most remote areas, are fully booked.

GIBB RIVER ROAD

This unmade road leads to the best-known gorges in Devonian Reef, the main attractions in the Kimberley region. They are, however, only motorable in the dry season, i.e. not between December and April.

The Gibb River Road should only be tackled in a 4×4. Inform yourself beforehand about its condition at the *Main Road Department (tel. 08 9158 43 33)* (detailed information can also be found on the Internet under *www.derbytourism.com. au*). A number of cattle stations in the vicinity provide accommodation, e.g **INSIDER TIP** *Digger's Rest (campsite with cabins | tel. 08 9161 10 29 | www.diggers rest.com | Budget)*.

KUNUNURRA

(158 A4) (MUD2) **This small town (pop. 6000) on the border to Northern Territory, was only built in the 1960 during the construction of the massive Ord River dam.**

Boat-trips are offered on *Lake Argyle*, the reservoir that was created covering more than 386mi². The best-known place to stay, some 100km (62mi) away, is in *El Questro Wilderness Park* which has a variety of different types of accommodation

The Gibb River Road is only passable at certain times of the year

ranging from the 5-star Homestead to a campsite open May–October. The ideal starting point for tours in Kimberley with spectacular scenery guaranteed *(www. elquestro.com.au)*.

INFORMATION

KUNUNURRA VISITOR CENTRE
Coolibah Drive | tel. 08 91 68 11 77 | www. kununurratourism.com

WHERE TO GO

PURNULULU NATIONAL PARK
(158 A5) (⑭ D2)
A visit to this national park is only possible in the dry season, from around May–September. First discovered as a

tourist destination in the 1980s, the striped *Bungle Bungle Range* sandstone formations in various shades are 300km (186mi) south of Kununurra and are just as spectacular as Uluru (Ayers Rock). From the Great Northern Road the park can only be reached by 4×4s even in good weather (dirt track crossing several watercourses). Information: *Halls Creek Tourist Centre | Hall Street | tel. 08 9168 62 62 | www.hallscreektourism.com.au*

MARGARET RIVER

(170 B5) (⑭ B6) This delightful small town is the centre of a still very young but already renowned wine-growing region.
There are some 100 wineries, with wine-tasting available in many. Some also have excellent restaurants. Paths lead through lovely woods; wonderful beaches with sensational surfing can be found along the rocky coast between Cape Naturaliste and Cape Leeuwin, with more sheltered bathing spots around sandy Geographe Bay. Between June–December whales visit the coastal waters and, with a bit of luck, you can sometimes see them from the shore.

FOOD & DRINK

COLONIAL BREWING COMPANY
Various types of tasty home-brewed beer including *Kolsch Ale,* that is very similar to the German beer of a similar name. Available in bottles to take away or to be drunk in the pub or its lovely beer garden. Live music Sunday lunchtimes. *Osmington Rd. | tel. 08 97 58 81 77 | www.colonialbrewing co.com.au | daily 10am–6pm | Budget– Moderate*

MARGARET RIVER

MARGARET RIVER CHOCOLATE COMPANY

A must for the sweet-toothed, a treat for fans of all things spicy. In this small factory, the delicious chocolate is also mixed with exotic spices, e.g. with chili pepper. *Corner Harman's Mill/Harman's South Road | www. chocolatefactory.com.au*

WINE

The *Regional Wine Centre (9, Bussel Highway, www.mrwines.com)* provides a good overview of the location of local wineries and the wines they produce. A tasting session (and lunch) can be recommended at Hamelin Bay Wines (McDonald Road, Karridale, approx. 32km/20mi to the

Wine-lovers will find what they're looking for in the area around Margaret River

SHOPPING

ART

A considerable number of artists and craftspeople have settled in this attractive area. Most studios and galleries are between Margaret River and Yallingup or Dunsborough. A small selection of exquisite, high-quality objects is on sale in *Yallingup Galleries (Caves/Gunyulgup Valley Road)*, including works by the contemporary artist Judy Prosser with her unusual Aboriginal motifs. For further addresses, see: *www.margaretriverartisans.co.au.*

south), with a beautiful view from the terrace, and in the stylish winery *Leeuwin Estate (Steven Road)* which has an art gallery and an excellent restaurant.

WHERE TO STAY

QUEST MARGARET RIVER

Spacious 1–3 roomed self-catering flats in the centre of the town but quietly located, with a swimming pool and bar. *90 rooms, Bussell Highway/Tunbridge Street, tel. 08/97572033, www.questmargaret river.com.au | Moderate–Expensive*

VISITOR CENTRE
Bussel Highway | tel. 08 97 57 20 11 | www. margaratriver.com

WHERE TO GO

BUNBURY
(170 B5) (*ψ B6*)
The old port area in this coastal town in the northeast *(www.visitbunbury.com.au)* has been remodelled and now includes an attractive apartment complex with holiday flats *(Mantra Bunburry | 64 rooms, pool and spa | tel. 08 92 67 48 88 | www. mantra.com.au | Moderate-Expensive)* restaurants, bars and shops. The main attraction are the some 100 dolphins in the bay. Many pop up next to the boat during the *Dolphin Watch Eco Tour* organised by naturalists *(Naturaliste Charters | from Dolphin Discovery Centre | Koombana Drive | daily 11am and 3pm, duration 90 mins. | tel. 08 97 95 22 76 | www.dolphin discovery.com.au | A$55).*

BUSSELTON (170 B5) (*ψ B6*)
Soft white sandy beaches have made this welcoming coastal town a popular place for a summer break. There are enough good places to stay *(Geographe Bay Holiday Park* on the beach *| 525 Bussell Highway | tel. 08 97 52 43 96 | www.geographebay holidaypark.com.au | Budget–Moderate)* and restaurants *(The Equinox | tel. 08 97 52 46 41,* or *The Goose Café | tel. 08 97 54 77 00,* both with a view of the ocean *| Moderate)* to be able to spend a few relaxing days right on *Geographe Bay*. The pier that extends 1.8km (more than 1mi) into the water is the longest in the Southern Hemisphere. A small railway along its length takes you to the underwater observatory *(daily guided tours on the hour 9am–4pm | www.busseltonjetty.com.au |*

A$30) where you can get up close to the sea life in the bay. Information: *www. geographebay.com*

CAPE LEEUWIN
(170 B5) (*ψ B6*)
Bussel Highway leads to the infamous rocky headland in the south feared by seafarers and battered by breakers. Beyond Augusta, the last settlement of any size, the tall slim 🔦 lighthouse comes into sight. If you take a guided tour, you will hear some thrilling stories about this monumental maritime building from 1896 and can climb up to the lookout running all around with breath-taking, far-reaching views *(daily 9am–5pm, reservations: tel. 08 97 57 74 11)*. There are two campsites in the vicinity: *Flinders Bay Caravan Park (Albany Terrace | tel. 08 91 58 13 80 | www.flindersbaypark.com.au)* on the sea in a sheltered bay, but with no views, and *Turner Caravan Park (1 Blackwood Avenue | tel. 08 97 58 15 93)* in an equally sheltered estuary on the edge of the *Leeuwin National Park*.

CAPE NATURALISTE LIGHTHOUSE
(170 B6) (*ψ B6*)
The massive lighthouse and the maritime museum document the adventurous seafaring history here in Geographe Bay. A guided tour also includes the platform around the lantern room where you gaze far out into the Indian Ocean. Between September and December whales can be seen. Fancy a luxury place to stay in the middle of nowhere? The exclusive *Hidden Valley Retreat*, with four secluded eco chalets scattered around the bushland, guarantees absolute privacy. Only those who don't want to cook dinner themselves get a visit from the chef who conjures up a gourmet meal *(approx. 50km/31mi southeast | Hagg Road | tel. 08 97 55 10 66 | www.yourhiddenvalley.com | Expensive)*.

A distinctive silhouette: modern buildings dominate the skyline in Perth

LIMESTONE CAVES
(170 B5) (*M B6*)

There are about 330 caves in the karst landscape around Margaret River. The few that can be accessed are on Caves Road. Before you disappear underground, visit the *Caveworks Visitor Centre (daily 9am–5pm | www.margaretriver.com)* 25km (15½mi) to the south where displays, films and animations provide comprehensive information on the caves and their fragile ecosystem.

The main subterranean attraction is the *Jewel Cave (35km/22mi south | daily 9.30am–4pm | A$19)*, simply on account of its glittering illuminations that are turned on at the flick of a switch. Guided tours to the sound of a didgeridoo are more adventurous through the more natural world of stalactites and stalagmites in *Ngilgi Cave (Yallingup, 45km/28mi north | daily 9.30am–4.30pm | tel. 08/97552152, A$20)*.

PERTH

MAP ON PAGE 107
(170 B4) (*M B6*) **The modern capital of Western Australia (pop. 1.7 million) is on the Swan River, some 15 km (9mi) upriver from the port of Fremantle.** The city centre has an interesting mixture of elegant buildings in the colonial style and ultra-modern glass and concrete structures. *Cottesloe Beach*, some 8km (5mi) southwest of the centre, the best-known beach in Western Australia, can be reached by bus and train.

SIGHTSEEING

FREMANTLE
Beautiful, restored buildings give Perth's port a special charm of its very own. Good restaurants *(e.g. on Fishing Boat Harbour)* and cafés on South Street, shops and

markets *(Victoria Market Hall, corner Henderson/South Terrace, Fri 9am–9pm, Sat 9am–5pm, Sun 10am–5pm)* attract visitors – either by train or boat from *Swan Bell Tower/Barrack Street Jetty* in Perth. Information: *Fremantle Tourist Bureau | Kings Square High Street | tel. 08 94 31 78 78 | www.fremantlewa.com.au*

KINGS PARK

Just a few minutes from the city centre, the park is an oasis of peace for those tired from walking everywhere. Lovely panoramic views from ⊿⊾ *Kings Park Lookout* and *DNA Observation Tower.*

PERTH MINT

This is where you can see the world's largest collection of gold nuggets and watch while the metal is cast. *310 Hay Street | Mon–Fri 9am–5pm, Sat/Sun 9am–1pm | A$8*

> **CITY** **WHERE TO START?**
> Many sights can be reached on foot from the pedestrianised City Mall *(Murray/Hay St.)* including the pretty banks of the Swan River with the sound of The Swan Bells and the railway station, where regional trains also stop, e.g. from Fremantle. The bus terminal is opposite the station. For drivers, park on the side of the road (parking metres) or in one of the multi-storey carparks *(e.g. Central Park, 152–158 Georges Terrace).*

THE SWAN BELLS

Bells modelled on those in London's famous church St Martin-in-the-Fields can be heard ringing from the tower *(daily except Wed and Fri noon and 1pm).*

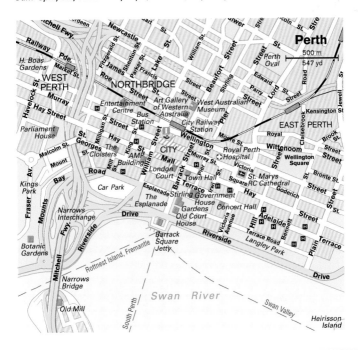

Barrack Sq./Riverside Drive | daily 10am–4.30pm | A$7 | www.swanbells.com.au

WESTERN AUSTRALIAN MUSEUM
The museum provides a good idea of the history of this colony. *Francis Street | daily 9.30am–5pm | admission free | www.museum.wa.gov.au*

FOOD & DRINK

EMPEROR'S COURT
The restaurant is considered by many to be the best Chinese restaurant in the whole of Western Australia. *66 Lake Street Northbridge | tel. 08 93 28 88 60 | open every day | Moderate*

INSIDER TIP FRASER'S RESTAURANT
Excellent fish, together with great views of Kings Park and the city. *Fraser Avenue | Kings Park | tel. 08 94 81 71 00 | open every day | Moderate*

OLD SWAN BREWERY
A wide choice of dishes and home-made beer are served in this restaurant on the river. *173 Mounts Bay RoadCrawley | tel. 08 92 11 89 99 | open every day | Moderate*

SHOPPING

A large selection of shops and arcades can be found in the area around *St Georges Terrace* and in *William Street, Wellington Street* and *Barrack Street.*

ENTERTAINMENT

'Xpress' – Perth's free magazine that appears every Thursday *(www.xpressmag.com.au)* – lists everything that is hip and which live bands are appearing where. Nightlife is largely concentrated in INSIDER TIP *Subiaco (Hay Street).*

C-RESTAURANT
Revolving restaurant in the 33rd floor with a cosy lounge; great sunsets. *Level 33 | 44 St Georges Terrace | Sun–Fri 11am–midnight, Sun 5pm–midnight*

INSIDER TIP MUST WINE BAR
The incredible winelist offers a choice of 40 different wines by the glass and 500 by the bottle. French snacks also served. *519 Beaufort Street | www.must.com.au | open every day*

WHERE TO STAY

BILLABONG BACKPACKERS RESORT
New, comfortable, cheap hotel. *56 rooms | 381 Beaufort Street | tel. 08 93 28 77 20 | www.billabongresort.com.au | Budget*

INSIDER TIP FREMANTLE COLONIAL ACCOMMODATION
3 charming cottages in the centre as well as a B&B (4 rooms). *215 High Street | tel. 08 94 30 65 68 | www.fremantlecolonial accommodation.com.au | Moderate–Expensive*

INFORMATION

WESTERN AUSTRALIAN TOURIST CENTRE
Forrest Place/Wellington St. | tel. (toll-free in Australia) 1300 36 13 51 | www.western australia.com | www.perth.citysearch.com.au

WHERE TO GO

KALGOORLIE-BOULDER
(175 E3) (*ɯ C5*)
Some 600km (373mi) away, a trip from Perth to the goldfields in the east is more than a mere excursion. Discovered in 1892, the gold reserves are still one of the main reasons for the affluence of Western

Australia. The area is characterised by open-cut mines. For information on tours: *Kalgoorlie-Boulder Tourist Centre | tel. 08 90 21 19 66 | www.kalgoorlie.com*

PINNACLES (NAMBUNG) NATIONAL PARK ★ (170 B3) *(ω A5)*

A paradise for photographers. The spectacular collection of up to 5m (16ft)-high

granules of the sand blown by the wind solidified into limestone columns on which more sand became stuck.

ROTTNEST ISLAND (170 B4) *(ω B6Y)*

The 11km (7mi)-long and 5km (3mi)-wide island, 18km (11mi) from Perth is a good weekend destination. Ferry companies offer tours lasting one or several days to

Pinanacles National Park

limestone pillars, 260km (162mi) north of Perth, is best visited early in the morning for perfect light conditions. Lot's wife could possibly have met her fate as described in the Bible if the rocks here were of salt, as at least some of the Pinnacles look like people turned to stone. If you take the 5km (3mi) circuit route through the forest of pillars or pose for a photo between the boulders, one really can believe in such a story. It has been worked out that the Pinnacles were created some 150,000–80,000 years ago. The sun baked hollow trunk-like formations in the desert. Through a chemical reaction, the

the island that is known for its interesting natural history. Information: *Rottnest Island Visitor Centre | tel. 08 93 72 97 52 | www.rottnestisland.com*

WAVE ROCK ★
(175 D4) *(ω B6)*

An imposing rock formation shaped like a 15m (49ft)-high wave, 350km (217mi) southeast of Perth near Hyden. This huge and bizarre wave was created by the wind and weather, heat, frost and flood waters that in the course of time left their mark in the form of strange striped patterns. Wave Rock is more than 2 million years old.

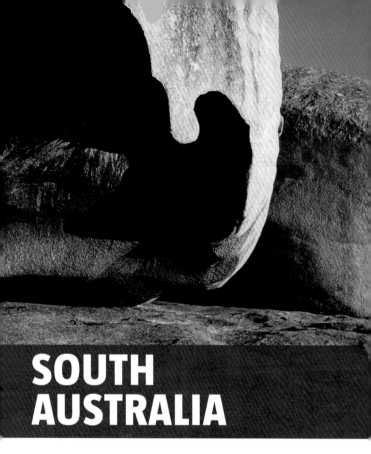

SOUTH AUSTRALIA

South Australia means undiluted adventure in the outback. Around 1.7 million people live in this state that covers just under 386,000mi².

Most live in the attractive and cultivated capital, Adelaide, and in the fertile plains around South Australia's life-giving artery, the huge Murray River. In the agricultural areas in the south, vines, fruit and cereals are grown. In the west and north these soon give way to extensive cattle and sheep farming regions and then into arid zones and fascinating desert. There are hidden oases almost all over the place which have a great variety of plants and animals. After rare but often heavy rainfall everything bursts into life even in the driest of areas. Carpets of wild flowers shoot up, insects buzz about and birds collect around the suddenly created lakes and ponds. And the number of kangaroos, dingos and small marsupials multiplies during such periods of plenty before the water disappears again.

ADELAIDE

MAP INSIDE BACK COVER
(175 D6) *(⋔ F6)* ★ Elegant, historical sandstone buildings set in flowering gardens, wide lawned areas and

Desert, wine and broad horizons: red sand, spikey spinifex grass and bizarre rock formations

well-tended parks – the city was carefully planned by immigrants.

No convicts came to South Australia. Many of the first European settlers who arrived in the first half of the 19th century were people who had to leave their native countries for religious or political reasons. Adelaide is a tolerant, multi-cultural and cultivated city with numerous museums, theatres and concert halls.

> **CITY** **WHERE TO START?**
> **Victoria Square** is the starting point if you fancy something to eat in the gastro scene on Grote St., want to take the tram to Glenelg, or don't mind the 10-minute walk to North Terrace, the first address for the city's main attractions.

SIGHTSEEING

ADELAIDE BOTANIC GARDEN
Peaceful park with lakes and a beautiful tropical rainforest glasshouse. *North Terrace | daily 9am–sunset, free guided*

GLENELG
The tram from Victoria Square to the most popular beach in Adelaide takes approx. 20 mins. Catamarans run by *Temptation Sailing* leave from Holdfast Marina, just 5 mins. from the tram stop, for 3½-hour

This skeleton of a grey whale is in the South Australian Museum

tours daily 10.30am from Schomburk Pavilion | www.environment.sa.gov.au/ botanicgardens

ART GALLERY OF SOUTH AUSTRALIA
Australian and international art, changing touring exhibitions. *North Terrace | daily 10am–5pm, guided tours 11am and 2pm | admission free*

AYERS HOUSE HISTORIC MUSEUM
The building, constructed in 1845 by the erstwhile prime minister Sir Henry Ayers and filled with his Victorian furniture, is an excellent example of the colonial style of that time. *288 Northern Terrace | Tue–Fri 10am–4pm, Sat/Sun 1pm–4pm | A$8*

tours when you can swim with the dolphins *(from A$100, spectators only: from A$60, tel. 04 12 81 18 38, www.dolphinboat.com.au).*

MIGRATION MUSEUM
The museum throws light on the history of immigrants to South Australia up to the present day. *82 Kintore Avenue | Mon–Fri 10am–5pm, Sat/Sun 1pm–5pm | admission free (donations welcome)*

NATIONAL WINE CENTRE
The futuristic Wine Centre building is on the edge of the Botanic Garden. Interactive displays tell you everything you want to know about the wines of South Australia that is especially well known for

its earthy, spicy reds. The Centre has an excellent cellar where rare Australian wines can also be bought. *Yarrabee House | Botanic Road | wine tasting daily 10am–5.30pm | www.wineaustralia.com.au*

PORT ADELAIDE

The historical port district in the northwest of the city keeps the city's early beginnings alive. The brochure 'Walk the Port' from the visitor centre is a useful guide for a walk through the restored streets as well as for the lighthouse, erected in 1868 down on the water, or the South Australia Maritime Museum *(126 Lipson St., daily 10am–5pm, A$8)* which is well worth visiting.

SOUTH AUSTRALIAN MUSEUM

The Ingarnendi Collection in the natural history museum traces the everyday life of Australia's indigenous people, their culture, spirituality and medical progress since the arrival of the first European settlers. *North Terrace | daily 10am–5pm | free guided tours Mon–Fri 11am, Sat/Sun 2pm and 3pm | www.samuseum.sa.gov.au*

TANDANYA – NATIONAL ABORIGINAL CULTURAL INSTITUTE

The cultural institute of the Kuarna Aborigines has art and craft galleries and changing exhibitions. A variety of guided tours are offered (from 40 mins. to half a day), for which reservations must be made 7 days in advance, and also includes a *cultural performance* Tue–Sun at noon. Information under *www.tandanya.com.au. | 253 Grenfell Street | daily 10am–5pm*

FOOD & DRINK

The *Central Market* and neighbouring *Gouger Street* have the biggest selection of restaurants and cafés. *Rundle Street* in the city centre is an alternative, as is *Melbourne Street* or *O'Connell Street* in the north and *Hutt Street* in the south.

BLISS ORGANIC CAFÉ

Restaurant with vegetarian dishes and freshly pressed fruit juices. *Compton St. | tel. 08 82 31 01 05 | closed Sun | Budget*

THE HILTON

First-class dishes, made exclusively with produce from South Australia, are served in INSIDER TIP *The Brasserie (open every day | Moderate)*, whereas *The Grange (closed Sun–Tue | Moderate–Expensive)* is known more for its fusion cooking. *223 Victoria Square | in the Hilton hotel | tel. 08 82 17 20 00*

THE MANSE

Stylishly furnished restaurant with modern European-Australian food. *142 Tynte St. |*

North Adelaide | tel. 08 82 67 46 36 | closed afternoons and Sun | *Expensive*

SHOPPING

Adelaide is good for opals, outback clothing, craft items and Aboriginal art. *Rundle Mall* is the shopping centre with department stores, boutiques, café and arcades, as is King William Road (Hyde Park) and the *Jam Factory Contemporary Craft & Design* (19 Morphett Street).

CENTRAL MARKET
The market which is roofed over has more than 80 stands with vegetables, fruit, fish and meat from the area. Asian and European dishes can be sampled at small stands. *Tue, Thu, Fri and Sat | Grote Street | www.adelaidecentralmarket.com.au*

ENTERTAINMENT

The supplement in the 'Adelaide Advertiser' on Thursdays gives a good summary of plays, concerts, operas, musicals and exhibitions. Tickets for many events can be booked through BASS *(tel. 13 12 46 | www.bass.net.au)*. The premier original live music venues are *Fowlers Live (68 North Terrace | www.fowlerslive.com.au)* and *Enigma* (rock) *(Thu–Sat | 173 Hindley Street | www.enigmabar.com.au)*. Cultural events can be found under *www.bcl.com.au/adelaide/wotson.htm.* In the South Australian Visitor and Travel Centre there is a free *HIP Guide to Adelaide* that gives reliable and up-to-date tips.

WHERE TO STAY

GLENELG BEACH HOSTEL
The award-winning backpacker hostel is in a wonderful and particularly attractive old building in the beach suburb of Glenelg. *30 rooms | 1–7 Mosely Square | tel. 08*

83 76 00 07 | www.glenelgbeachhostel. com.au | *Budget*

INSIDER TIP NORTH ADELAIDE HERITAGE GROUP COTTAGES
7 beautifully restored cottages and other heritage properties with period-style beds scattered around the city centre and North Adelaide and run on a B&B basis. Pick the one that best suits you: *tel. 08 82 72 13 55 | www.adelaideheritage.com | Expensive*

INFORMATION

SOUTH AUSTRALIAN VISITOR AND TRAVEL CENTRE
18 King William Street | tel. 08 83 03 20 33 | www.southaustralia.com

WHERE TO GO

ADELAIDE HILLS
(175 D6) (*ᗰ F6*)
The gently rolling landscape of the Adelaide Hills *(www.adhills.com.au)* starts some 30km (19mi) from Adelaide. 50 Lutheran migrant families who arrived in South Australia aboard the ship 'Zebra', founded the village of *Hahndorf* (pop. 1700) in 1839. Half-timbered, German-style houses, an old German butcher's, a German inn, an antique clock museum and numerous souvenir shops and restaurants attract lots of tourists to Hahndorf every year.

BAROSSA VALLEY ★
(175 D6) (*ᗰ F6*)
Excellent wines, rye bread, sourdough, cheese, olives, smoked sausages and ham – and historical villages in pretty countryside: this is Barossa, a must for wine-lovers. Located some 55km (34mi) northeast of Adelaide, there are more than 50 wineries. The first British farmers set-

tled in the Barossa area in 1840 and, from 1842, Lutherans from Silesia, Brandenburg and Posen (Prussia, now Poland) arrived and found a new home here that was tolerant to their religious beliefs. They brought the first vines with them to this now world-famous wine-growing region. The first German settlement, *Bethany*, is a traditional elongated village with houses on one side of the road and small fields on the other.

Tanunda (population 3500) is a good starting point for a ● wine and gourmet tour through the region. It's a good idea to stay at least one night here, e.g. in *Blickinstal B&B (Rifle Range Road | Tanunda | tel. 08 85 63 27 16 | www.blickinstal.com.au | Moderate)* which has 6 cosy rooms, a view over the vineyards and hearty breakfasts. Information: *Barossa Wine & Visitor Centre (66–68 Murray Street | Tanunda | tel. 08 85 63 06 00 | www.barossa.com).* Here you can also pick up the *Winery Map* with a description of the *Scenic Drive 4* through the Barossa Valley. It is well worth stopping at the wineries on Para Road as well as at Seppelt, Penfolds, Charles Melton, Bethany Wines and Villa Tinto.

CLARE VALLEY

(175 D6) (*ﾉﾉ F6*)

Another idyllic wine-growing region, 140km (87mi) to the north of Adelaide and, as such, a full day's tour if you want to visit one or other prize-winning winery and have a delicious lunch in lovely surroundings. *Knappstein Wines (2 Pioneer Avenue | Mon–Fri 9am–5pm, Sat 11am–5pm, Sun 11am–4pm | tel. 08 88 42 26 00 | www.knappsteinwines.com.au)* vouches for the very best quality wines, both red and white. At *Skillogalee Wines (daily 10am–5pm | tel. 08 88 43 43 11 | www.skillogalee.com)* you don't just get a light Riesling to drink but delicious lunch-

Wine has been produced in Barossa for more than 150 years

es are also served. Those with at least one more day on their hands can explore the wine-growing area between *Auburn* and *Clare* by bike along the *Riesling Trail*. Bikes can be hired, luggage forwarded if so desired, as can any wine bought en route. *(Clare Valley Visitor Information Centre | corner Main North/Spring Gully Road | Clare | tel. 1800 24 21 31 | www.claregilbert valleys.sa.gov.au). 120km (75mi) north of Adelaide*

In Flinders Ranges National Park

INSIDER TIP **EYRE PENINSULA**
(174 B5) (*Ø E–F6*)

Wonderful coastline with fine sandy beaches are the trademark of this peninsula 500km (310mi) west of Adelaide. The desert plains and outback of the Gawler Ranges and the dried up salt lake *Lake Gairdner* can be found further inland. Kangaluna Camp, a comfortable site, is at the centre. From here it is around a 2-hour drive to Baird Bay where you can swim with the sea lions and dolphins. Information on tours: *www.gawlerranges safaris.com.au*

FLEURIEU PENINSULA
(174 C6) (*Ø F6*)

For the people of Adelaide the peninsula is an attractive recreational area for day-trippers with sheltered beaches especially on the northwest. Inland, around rural *McLaren Vale,* there are more than 65 wineries in this renowned wine-growing region *(www.producers.net.au).* The local visitor centre *(Main Road | tel. 08 83 23 99 44 | www.tourismvictorharbour.com. au)* can point those interested in wine-tasting in the right direction. *Goolwa* on *Lake Alexandrina* is popular: a lovely beach, lots of restaurants and places to stay and the possibility to explore the *Coorong National Park* on a boat-trip *(Coorong Cruises | tel. 08 85 55 22 03 | www.coorong cruises.com.au). Victor Harbor (12 000 pop. | www.tourismvictorharbor.com.au)* is also very popular. The *South Australian Whale Centre (2 Railway Terrace | daily 11am–4.30pm | A\$8)* with information on the Southern Right Whales, that can be watched here from June–September, is particularly interesting. *Granite Island* off Victor Harbour is home to around 2000 tiny Fairy Penguins. The island can be reached across a wooden bridge on foot or on the historical horse-drawn tram. Accommodation is available in *Cape Jervis Station (15 rooms | Cape Jervis Rd. | flats, B&B and holiday houses | tel. 08 85 98 02 88 | www.capejervisstation.com.au | Moderate).* 100km (62mi) south

FLINDERS RANGES NATIONAL PARK ★
(175 D3) (*Ø F5–6*)

The bizarre rock formations that shimmer in reds and violets above the expanse of the plain more than 400km (250mi) north of Adelaide make up this national park that covers 370mi². Deep gorges cut through this largely arid region. Most tours and places to stay in this fantastic wilderness have to be booked beforehand in Adelaide. A 4×4 is only needed if you leave the main route. *Wilpena Pound*, a huge area surrounded by jagged rocks, is the most characteristic landmark of the Flinders Ranges. More than 500 million years ago, this plateau was part of the seabed. Numerous fossils testify to this.

INSIDER TIP *Iga Warta (tel. 08 86 48 37 37 | www.igawarta.com)* is owned by the Coulthard family who tell visitors about the culture of the Adnyamathanha people. Cliff Coulthard, who helped in the safeguarding and interpretation of the cave paintings in Lascaux, France, shows his guests some of the many rock paintings and engravings in the gorges of the Flinders Ranges. Guests help hunt and collect bush food, hike through the peaceful countryside or ride out on the family's horses into the heart of the mountains. Tours can last from just a few hours to several days (from A$30). You can camp at Iga Warta (via Copley) or be picked up

island is a must for a animal-lovers. You can reach Kangaroo Island by air from Adelaide *(flight time approx. 30 mins., Regional Express/Rex | tel. 13 17 13, www. rex.com.au* or *Air South | tel. 08 82 34 49 88 | www.airsouth.com.au)* or cross on the car ferry (approx. 1 hour) from Cape Jervis on Fleurieu Peninsula to Penneshaw *(Kangaroo Island Sealink Ferry | tel. 13 13 01 | www.sealink.com.au | car and 2 people approx. A$330).*

There is no public transport on the island. More than half of Kangaroo Island is dense-

Gammons Ranges, Iga Warta, rock drawings

at *Wilpena Pound Resort (60 rooms | 400 pitches for tents | tel. 08 86 48 00 04 | www. wilpenapound.com.au | Moderate).*

KANGAROO ISLAND ★
(174 C6) *(∅ F6–7)*
Kangaroo Island is 120km (75mi) southwest of Adelaide. The 150km (93mi)-long

ly forested; more than 30% of the bushland is a national park. Huge colonies of seals and sea lions occupy the beaches. Accompanied by rangers, a colony of several hundred sea lions can be visited in *Seal Bay Conservation Park (guided tours daily from 9am)* on *Seal Bay* in the south. Penguins nest right next to where the ferry comes in. In the evenings, pelicans crowd around the pier in *Kingscote*. In the winter, Southern Right Whales rest out at sea. Those who don't just want to hike or animal-watch, can swim, surf, dive, ride and cycle on Kangaroo Island, stock up on honey and eucalyptus oil products – and eat very well too. You can stay the night for example in cabins at *Flinders Chase Farm (tel. 08 85 59 72 23 | Budget)* or in the *The Kings B&B (deluxe suite with ocean view | American River | tel. 08 85 53 70 03 | Moderate)*.

Day-trips from Adelaide by bus and ferry last approx. 16 hours. One possibility is to travel by bus (leaving at around 6.30am), returning by air at around 6pm *(organ-* ised by Sealink | www.sealink.com.au)* or, better still, plan 2 days for the island. Good natural history tours available through *APT (tel. 08 85 53 03 86, www.kiodysseys.com. au)*, also if driving yourself. Comprehensive information under: *www.tourkangaroo island.com.au*

COOBER PEDY

(174 A2) (⟨fi⟩ E5) **Located on the Stuart Highway 846km (526mi) north of Adelaide and 685km (426mi) from Alice Springs. Coober Pedy (Aboriginal kuba piti for 'white man's hole'), is famous for the while opal found in the area.**

The entire area is peppered with thousands of little mine shafts. 85% of the opals used for jewellery come from Coober Pedy and the two other opal towns *Andamooka* and *Mintabie*. With temperatures during the day topping 45°C (113°F) and freezing cold nights, it is not a surprise that the 3500 residents of Coober Pedy have made a virtue of out necessity with many living is disused mines. Whole houses and even churches and hotels have been carved out of the rock. In these so-called dugouts, the temperature remains a pleasant 24°C (75°F) all year round.

The *mail run* that goes from Coober Pedy *(Mon–Thu 9am)* to *Oodnadatta* and *William Creek (600km/373mi in approx. 12 hours | approx. A$195 | tel. 08 86 72 52 26 | www.desertdiversity.com.au)* provides a good insight into life in the out-back and its scenery. A one-hour sightsee-ing flight takes you to the INSIDER TIP *Anna Creek Painted Hills*, a hilly sandstone area approx. 116mi² in size, that shimmers spec-tacularly in various colours *(from Coober Pedy or William Creek approx. A$250, www.wrightsair.com.au)*.

Opals from Coober Pedy are cheaper in this mining town than anywhere else in the country

SIGHTSEEING

OLD TIMERS MINE

Tours are run to these former opal mines. 2 dugout houses can also be visited. *Crowders Gully Rd.* | *daily 9am–5pm* | *A$8*

FOOD & DRINK

TOM & MARY'S TAVERNA

Greek restaurant. *Hutchison Street* | *tel. 08 86 72 56 22* | *open every day* | *Budget*

SHOPPING

Shops in Hutchison Street work opals and sell jewellery. Prices here are lower than in cities *(www.cooberpedyopal.com.au)*.

WHERE TO STAY

RADEKA'S DUGOUT BACKPACKERS

The *Inn & Underground Motel* has dugout accommodation to suit every budget, ranging from cheap bunks to underground family suites. *8 rooms* | *Oliver Road* | *tel. 08 86 72 52 23* | *www.radekadownunder. com.au* | *Budget–Moderate*

INFORMATION

VISITOR INFORMATION CENTRE

In the District Council building | *Hutchison Str.* | *tel. 1800 63 70 76* | *www.opalcapital oftheworld.com.au*

WHERE TO GO

THE BREAKAWAYS RESERVE

(174 B1) (*ØU E5*)

This colourful hilly area is some 32km (20mi) north of Coober Pedy. From time to time it is used as a film set. ☼ Panorama Hill for example played an important role in the action film 'Mad Max' made in 1979, that helped the Australian actor Mel Gibson to his international breakthrough.

TASMANIA

Almost one third of Tasmania's countryside is a protected area – craggy mountain peaks, huge ferns, giant trees covered with moss, fast-flowing streams, lakes and hidden beaches.

Cut off from mainland Australia, plants and animals have evolved here that cannot be found anywhere else. The main island is about 3 times the size of Wales and is the smallest and coldest state in Australia. Most of the some 520,000 inhabitants live in Hobart in the south and Launceston in the north. Tasmania can best be explored by car. Accommodation is generally expensive – one alternative is to rent a campervan (e.g. from Auto Rent Hertz, *www.autorent.com.au*). In summer, campsites should be booked in advance.

CRADLE MOUNTAIN/ LAKE ST CLAIR

(179 D5) (*ω G8*) ★ The Cradle Mountain/Lake St Clair National Park is one of the oldest nature reserves in Tasmania and a wonderful hiking area.

Photo: Wineglass Bay in Freycinet National Park

Untamed wilderness: the continent's smallest state is considered an insider tip by those who are frequent visitors to Australia

There are two entrances to the national park: in the south, Highway A10 turns off to Lake St Clair; in the north, a side road takes you to Cradle Valley. The latter has turned into a kind of centre for the park due to its infrastructure tailored to tourists' needs, whereas Lake St Clair boasts an untouched, romantic and peaceful shoreline. A park licence is need for cars and passengers *(approx. A$60 for up to 8 people).*

FOOD & DRINK
WHERE TO STAY

CRADLE MOUNTAIN LODGE

The rustic but stylishly furnished hotel complex is right next to the north entrance to the park. After a tiring hike you can relax in the adjoining *Waldheim Alpine Spa* and let yourself be pampered with a massage or other spa treatment, before dining in the well-known restaurant *(100 cabins | tel. 02 82 96 80 10 | www.cradle mountainlodge.com.au | Expensive)*.

CRADLE VALLEY DISCOVERY HOLIDAY PARKS
Cheap accommodation some 2km (1¼mi) from the northern entrance to the park. *Campervan pitches and 36 cabins | tel. 03*

Station, with a natural history display that is well worth seeing, just inside the north entrance, and Dove Lake. The 17km (10½mi) route, there and back, takes about 5 hours, past scrub covered in moss and giant trees. An alternative for those who don't want to walk the distance is the shuttlebus from the visitor centre through the park.

Circular walk around Lemonthyme Lodge

64 92 13 95 | www.discoveryholidayparks. com.au | Budget

INSIDER TIP▶ LEMONTHYME LODGE
About 25km (15½mi) outside the national park on the road to Moina. Guests are accommodated in 29 luxurious cabins in the middle of a wood. The restaurant in the wooden main building is exellent. *Cradle Mountain Road | tel. 03 64 92 11 12 | www.lemonthyme.com.au | Expensive*

SPORTS & ACTIVITIES

CRADLE VALLEY BOARDWALK
Well-maintained trail between the *Interpretation Centre* in the *National Park Ranger*

OVERLAND TRACK
This trail from Cradle Mountain to Lake St Clair is around 65km (40mi) long. Taking about 5 days, you will pass through mountainous areas, upland moor, rainforest and deep valleys with spectacular waterfalls. For information on guided tours see: *www.tas-ex.com or www.cradlehuts. com.au | Nov–April reservations essential (www.overlandtrack.com.au)*

INFORMATION

CRADLE MOUNTAIN VISITOR CENTRE
At the northern entrance to the park, 2km (1¼mi) from the gates | tel. 03 64 92 15 90 | www.parks.tas.gov.au

DEVONPORT

(179 D5) *(𝄞 H8)* **Devonport (population 25,000) is the gateway to Tasmania's rugged northwest. Car ferries that travel daily between Melbourne and Tasmania dock in the town's busy port.**

Reservations and information: www.spirit oftasmania.com.au

SIGHTSEEING

TIAGARRA TASMANIAN ABORIGINAL CULTURAL CENTRE

This centre explains the 35,000-year-old history of the Tasmanian Aborigines. Shop with Aboriginal art and a café. *Mersey Bluff on the way to the lighthouse | Mon–Sat 9am–5pm | A$10*

FOOD & DRINK

LUCAS' HOTEL

Good beer and fresh hearty food. *Latrobe, 9km (5½mi) south | 46 Gilbert Street | tel. 03 64 26 11 01 | open every day | Budget–Moderate*

INFORMATION

TASMANIAN TRAVEL AND INFORMATION

92 Formby Road | tel. 03 64 24 44 66 www. devonporttasmania.travel

WHERE TO GO

DELORAINE (179 D5) *(𝄞 H8)*

For gourmets, this rural town 50km (31mi) to the southeast is well worth a detour. ☺ *41° South Aquaculture*, a salmon farm 6km (4mi) further southwest, signposted on the Montana Road *(www.41south-aquaculture.com)*, farms this delicious fish without the use of any chemicals. The small

shop sells fresh salmon, smoked products and salmon paste. And if you fancy something sweet, head for *Honey Farm (approx. 20km/12½mi west, in Chudleigh | 39 Sorell Street | www.thehoneyfarm.com.au)*. The star among the many types of honey is the aromatic *Leatherwood Honey* from the pollen of local giant trees.

STANLEY (179 D4) *(𝄞 G8)*

Victorian buildings and small shops line the old main street in Stanley (pop. 540, 100km/62mi northwest) below *The Nut (Circular Head)*. The steep rock with a chair lift is a popular place for sightseers. Penguins and colonies of sea lions can be visited or else take a boat-trip into the jungle-like *Arthur River Wilderness. Stanley's on the Bay (15 Wharf Rd. | Budget–Moderate)* and *Julie and Patrick (2 Alexander Terrace | Budget)* are excellent restaurants, and the cabins at INSIDER TIP ▶ *Beachside Retreat*

MARCO POLO HIGHLIGHTS

★ Cradle Mountain/ Lake St Clair
Virtually untouched mountainous wilderness with superb hiking trails → p. 120

★ Port Arthur
Ruins with a gruesome past, surrounded by delightful scenery → p. 126

★ Strahan
Fishing village and the gateway to Tasmania's wilderness → p. 128

★ Franklin-Gordon Wild Rivers National Park
Discover this secrets of the rainforest with its ferns, lichens and tumbling streams → p. 129

right on the beach are a romantic hideaway *(4 rooms | 31 Church Street | tel. 03 64 58 13 50 | www.beachsideretreat.com | Moderate–Expensive)*. Information and reservations: *Stanley Visitor Information | 45 Main Road | tel. 03 64 58 13 30 | www.stanley.com.au*

HOBART

(179 D6) (∅ H8) The capital of Tasmania (pop. 210,000) with its many sandstone colonial buildings stretches from the picturesque harbour on Derwent River right up into the surrounding mountains.
The top of ⚛ Mount Wellington is often hidden in the mist or covered in snow. On clear days however you have a wonderful view of the city.

SIGHTSEEING

BATTERY POINT
Tiny historical workers' houses with front gardens full of flowers, old sandstone villas,

> **CITY WHERE TO START?**
> It's best not to drive into the city centre. **Sullivans Cove**, where tourist boats and ferries come in, is a suitable place to start a walk around the city centre and the historical districts Salamanca Place and Battery Point. If you come by bus, alight in the centre at Franklin Sq./Elisabeth St., not far from the Information Centre. It is 16km (10mi) from the airport by shuttle bus or taxi.

individual cafés, bookshops and antique shops are features of Hobart's oldest area around Hampden Road *(Arthur's Circus)*.

INSIDER TIP MONA (MUSEUM OF OLD AND NEW ART) ●
Visitors to this remarkable art museum on the banks of the River Derwent experience a real feast for the senses. Some stay for hours and can't get enough of the daring presentation of works of art varying

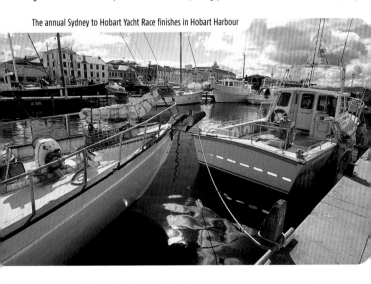
The annual Sydney to Hobart Yacht Race finishes in Hobart Harbour

from the established to the experimental. This collection is in private ownership and is the passion of a wealthy financial investor – and that's why it's (still) free! *655 Main Road | Berriedale | www.mona.net. au, Wed–Mon 10am–6pm*

BLUE EYE

Small restaurant with Italian-style cooking. Good value lunches. *Castray Esplanade/ Salamanca Place | tel. 03 62 23 52 97 | www.fishfish.com.au | lunch and dinner | Moderate–Expensive*

FISH FRENZY

An institution which always serves wonderfully fresh seafood. *Elisabeth Street Pier | tel. 03 62 31 21 34 | lunch and dinner | Moderate–Expensive*

MURES

Restaurant with its own fleet of fishing boats that also supplies other places in Hobart. Guests can choose between the elegant dining room on the first floor (*Moderate–Expensive*), a self-service area on the ground floor (*Budget–Moderate*), or a sushi bar (*Moderate–Expensive*). *Victoria Dock/Sullivans Cove, tel. 03 62 31 2121, www.mures.com.au, lunch and dinner*

PROSSER'S ON THE BEACH

Great fish dishes in a unique elevated position. *1 Beach Road Long Point Road (Sandy Bay) | tel. 03 62 25 22 76 | closed Sun | Expensive*

INSIDER TIP *Premier Travel Tasmania (tel. 03 62 27 13 88 | www.premiertraveltasma nia.com)* organises very good tours lasting several days for groups of at least 2 people, with a special emphasis on watching

Typical building in Battery Point

wildlife and exploring Tasmania's natural beauty.

LENNA OF HOBART

Luxury hotel in a listed villa. *50 rooms | 20 Runnymede Street | tel. 03 62 32 39 00 | www.lenna.com.au | Moderate*

SULLIVANS COVE APPARTMENTS

Spacious, smartly furnished self-catering rooms, most with a view of Sullivans Cove. *20 rooms | 19 A Hunter Street | tel. 03 62 34 50 63 | www.sullivanscoveappartments. com.au | Expensive*

TASMANIAN TRAVEL CENTRE

Davey Street corner Elizabeth Street | tel. 03 62 38 42 22 | www.hobarttravelcentre. com.au

WHERE TO GO

PORT ARTHUR ★ (179 E6) (*🗺 H8*)
The ruins of the penal colony are located on the picturesque Tasmanian Peninsula some 100km (62mi) south of Hobart. The interactive *Port Arthur Visitor Centre* and daily guided tours provide an insight into the everyday life of the convicts *(8.30am–5pm | Bronze Pass incl. guided tour and Harbour Cruise from A$30 | www.portarthur.org.au)*. You can rub shoulders with the local ghosts for A$22 during the 90-min. *Ghost Tour* held in the evening. The officers' quarters in this former penitentiary centre have been converted into 5 luxury holiday homes – the *Cascades Colonial Cottages* – located in an idyllic bay approx. 15km (9½mi) away *(533 Main Rd. | Koonya | tel. 03 62 50 38 73 | www.cascadescolonial.com.au | Moderate–Expensive)*.
Port Arthur Holiday Park is a deluxe campsite with large pitches and campfires *(tel. 03 62 50 23 40 | www.portarthurhp.com.au | book well in advance! | approx. 3km/2mi from the historic area)*. Approx. 10km (6mi) from Port Arthur (turn off beyond Koonya), is the *Tasmanian Devil Conservation Park,* where you have a particularly good opportunity to watch the carnivorous marsupials *(daily 9am–5pm | Port Arthur Highway, Taranna | www.tasmaniandevilpark.com)*.

LOW BUDGET

▶ The 90-min. trip around Hobart Harbour incl. lunch and wine costs A$28: *Captain Fell's Historic Ferries* cruise up the estuary of the Derwent River providing lovely views of the banks and a delicious meal *(tel. 03 62 23 58 93 | www.captainfellshistoricferries.com.au)*.

▶ Friday afternoons you can listen to ● live music in Rektango in the courtyard in historical Salamanca Place in Hobart – free of charge *(5.30pm–7.30pm)*.

LAUNCESTON

(179 D5) (*🗺 H8*) **Tasmania's second largest city (pop. 100,000) is a place that is very popular with gourmands.**
They don't just visit the many good restaurants but also the vineyards and fruit plantations in nearby Tamar Valley. Numerous historical buildings and parks can be found in Launceston city centre.

SIGHTSEEING

CATARACT GORGE
The deep gorge of the fast-flowing *South Esk River* reaches right into the heart of the city. A walk that lasts around 1 hour takes you across the swaying Alexandra suspension bridge up to the *Eagle Eyrie Lookout* and on to the old *Toll House* on *Kings Bridge.* A 1-hour boat-trip through the dramatic rocky gorge is equally enticing *(Tamar River Cruises | Home Point Cruise Terminal, at the end of Home Point Parade | tel. 03 63 34 99 00 | www.tamarrivercruises.com.au | daily 9.30am–5.30pm | A$24)*.

FOOD & DRINK

PIPER'S BROOK VINEYARD
Lunch surrounded by vineyards can be enjoyed in a number of wineries north of Launceston. Piper's Brook Vineyard has great food and lovely views from the restaurant terrace. *1216 Pipers Brook Road | www.pipersbrook.com | daily 10am–5pm | Budget–Moderate*

The remnants of an empire: Port Arthur, the former penal colony

STAR BAR CAFÉ
The best pizzas baked in a wood-fired oven are served behind this old façade. Live music Fri–Sun. *113 Charles Street | tel. 03 63 31 61 11 | open every day | Budget–Moderate*

INSIDER TIP STILLWATER
Trendy bistro with award-winning cuisine. *Ritchie's Mill | Patterson Street | tel. 03 63 31 41 53 | open every day | Expensive*

SPORTS & ACTIVITIES

HOLLYBANK TREETOP ADVENTURE
This adrenalin-kick at a dizzying height is undiluted, action-packed, outdoor fun. Attached to ropes, participants 'fly' over distances of up to 370m (1210ft). *Night Flights* take place in the dark. *15 mins. by car northeast | 66 Hollybank Road | Underwood | www.treetopsadventure.com.au | daily 9am–5pm | duration 3 hours incl. briefing.*

WHERE TO STAY

ALICE'S COTTAGES
Holiday cottages furnished in a variety of styles. If this is to your taste, you can find another 25 houses from the 19th and early 20th centuries dotted around Tasmania under **INSIDER TIP** *www.cottagesofthecolony.com.au. 129 Balfour Street | tel. 03 63 34 22 31 | www.cottagesofthecolony.com.au | Moderate–Expensive*

INFORMATION

LAUNCESTON TRAVEL AND INFORMATION CENTRE
12 John Street | tel. 03 63 36 31 33 | www.ltvtasmania.com.au

WHERE TO GO

BEAUTY POINT (179 E6) (𝑚 H8)
Some 50km (31mi) to the north, on the west bank of the wide Tamar River, three

attractions provide enough to do to fill a whole day. In the *Platypus House (www. platypushouse.com.au | A$20)* you can watch these shy creatures and echidnas at close quarters and then marvel at the delightful little creatures in *Seahorse World (www.seahorseworld.com.au | A$22)* next door *(Head Wharf | both from 9.30am, last guided tour 4.30pm)*. To the southwest, near *Beaconsfield,* the *Mine and Heritage Centre* provides an interesting insight into the history of Tasmania's largest gold mine *(West Street | www.beaconsfieldheritage. co.au | daily 9.30am–4.30pm | A$12)*. Reductions with the *Triple Pass (www. ltvtasmania.com.au)*. The *Beauty Point Tourist Park* campsite is peacefully situated on the water in the Tamar Valley *(36 West Arm Road | Beauty Point | tel. 03 63 83 45 36 | www.tasmaniantouristparks. com | Budget–Moderate)*.

ST HELENS

(179 E5) *(ω H8)* ⭐ **The former whaling station in sheltered Georges Bay has evolved into a lively holiday resort.**
There is a good selection of restaurants *(Blue Shed Café | tel. 03 63 76 11 70 | Moderate | fish can be bought next door)* and places to stay. Book in advance, even to stay on the campsites *(Camping Hillcrest | Stieglitz | approx. 6km/4mi | tel. 03 63 76 32 98)*. *Queechy Cottages* is a self-catering motel with a view of the bay, 5 mins. walk from the centre *(24 rooms | 2 Tasman Highway | tel. 03 63 76 13 21 | www.queechy cottages.com.au | Moderate)*. Information: *www.tasmaniaseastcoast.com.au*

WHERE TO GO

BAY OF FIRES (179 E6) *(ω H8)*
This elongated bay with dazzlingly white beaches, approx. 12km (7½mi) to the north, has isolated beaches to die for and wildly romantic campsites on the sea (Cosy Bag and Jeanneret Beach are especially beautiful), albeit without electricity. A detour to *Binalong Bay* is a must – even if only to have breakfast, lunch or dinner on the **INSIDER TIP** terrace with panoramic views at *Binalong Bay Café (64 A Main Rd. | tel. 03 6376811 | Budget–Moderate)*. Information: *www.binalongbay.com.au*

COLES BAY/ FREYCINET NATIONAL PARK
(179 E6) *(ω H8)*
A protected nature reserve to relax in with lonely sandy beaches – the beach in Wineglass Bay is considered as one of the most beautiful in the world (approx. 3-hour return walk from the carpark). Impressive views of the coast from the water. Take either a 4-hour *Eco Cruise* in a sleek catamaran *(tel. 03 62 57 03 55 | www. wineglassbaycruises.com.au)* or put your environmentally-friendly muscle power to the test in a kayak *(tel. 03 62 57 05 00 | www.freycinetadventures.com.au.*
🕐 *Freycinet Lodge (60 rooms, tel. 03 62 57 01 01 | www.freycinetlodge.com.au | Expensive)* is a luxurious place to stay. The lovely drinks terrace, with its wonderful view over Coles Bay, is also open to non-residents. Information under *www. freycinetcolesbay.com* and *www.parks. tas.gov.au.*

STRAHAN

(179 D5) *(ω G8)* ⭐ **Strahan (pop. 700) is a collection of small, pretty houses built of wood or brick.** Fishing boats, yachts and cruise boats for day-trippers bob around in Macquarie Harbour – a natural haven surrounded by hills. Strahan was once a penal colony and was later settled by lumberjacks.

Remote wilderness: the Franklin-Gordon Wild Rivers National Park

FOOD & DRINK WHERE TO STAY

STRAHAN VILLAGE

A variety of good accommodation is available right on the harbour. *140 rooms and flats | The Esplanade | tel. 03 64 71 42 00 | www.strahanvillage.com.au | Budget– Moderate*

ENTERTAINMENT

'The Ship that Never Was' is a humorous play about a successful escape from the penal colony. For some time now it has been enacted every day at around 5.30pm in the *theatre in Strahan Visitor Centre. Tickets A$14*

INFORMATION

STRAHAN VISITOR CENTRE

The Esplanade | tel. 03 64 72 68 00 | www.strahanvillage.com.au | www.western wilderness.com.au

WHERE TO GO

FRANKLIN-GORDON WILD RIVERS NATIONAL PARK ★ (179 D5–6) *(ɯ G8)*

Cruise from Macquarie Harbour up the Gordon River through one of the few temperate rainforests with trees up to 2000 years old (duration: approx. 6 hours). *Gordon River Cruises | The Esplanade | tel. 03 64 71 43 00 | www.strahanvillage. com.au*

QUEENSTOWN (179 D5) *(ɯ G8)*

This little mining town is located in the middle of a lunar landscape that is slowly being reafforested. Mainly copper and gold are mined here. Don't miss a visit to the historical *Paragon Theatre* that shows fascinating films on the countryside and history of the region *(daily from 2.45pm, last showing 6.30pm, www.theparagon. com.au)*. The *West Coast Wilderness Railway* runs twice daily along an adventurous 25km (16mi) stretch between Queenstown and Strahan *(www.puretasmania.com.au)*.

TRIPS & TOURS

The tours are marked in green in the road atlas, the pull-out map and on the back cover

① A JOURNEY THROUGH 'THE DREAMTIME'

The MacDonnell Ranges to the west and east of Alice Springs are one of the most important regions culturally for the central Australian Arrente Aborigines. A trip through the western section of the mountain range doesn't just take you to major 'Dreamtime' sites but also to breath-takingly beautiful gorges and a fascinating animal and plant kingdom. The tour can be completed in one day in a conventional car. However, it is well worth spending a night at the end of the tarmaced road to have enough time to soak up the spirit of the 'Dreaming' era.

The journey starts at Alice Springs → p. 84. 300m down Larapinta Drive on the left is the grave and memorial to John Flynn, the founder of the Royal Flying Doctor Service. After a further 10km (6mi), Simpsons Gap is a good place to stop for a break. A short path between mature eucalyptus trees leads to a small waterhole. Here you can see why Simpsons Gap and the other gorges in the MacDonnell Ranges are not only of cultural and spiritual importance to the local Aborigines but also life-giving. For thousands of years, they have found water and food

An adventurous tour through the wilderness and to Aboriginal sites and a gentle drive along the south coast

in this oasis in the middle of the parched desert. Continue on Larapinta Drive for another 24km (15mi) to **Standley Chasm** that plays an important role in the Termite Dreaming of the Iwupataka Aborigines. This gorge is especially spectacular at midday when the sun bathes the narrow corridor in a blazing red. After Standley Chasm, the road branches onto Namatjira Drive. After 42km (26mi), a turning to the right leads to **Ellery Creek Big Hole**. The geology of the area around the huge waterhole is particularly interesting and varied. Ellery Creek Big Hole is also one of the places in the western MacDonnell Ranges where camping is allowed. The trip continues along Namatjira Drive where you can stop at **Serpentine Gorge**. As the name suggests, the gorge snakes its way through the rocky landscape.

Don't miss a visit to Ochre Pits that present a cross-section through the 700 million-year-old geology of the region. Ochre from the pit faces that range in colour from bright yellow to rust red provided the local Aborigines with essential material for their rock paintings and was also used for trading purposes.

After a detour to Ormiston Gorge you reach Glen Helen Resort (25 rooms | Namatjira Drive | tel. 08 89 56 74 89 | www. glenhelen.com.au) which has a campsite and several cabins. Glen Helen is on the banks of the Finke River that has flowed along the same bed for 100 million years, reputedly making it the oldest river in the world. The waterhole is a paradise for birds in the region. The palm trees on the other side of the river were probably planted by Afghan camel drivers who played a decisive role in opening up a route into the heart of the continent.

If you are in a 4×4, you can carry on along the unsurfaced track and visit Redbank Gorge further to the west, where there is a lovely but basic campsite, before heading back to Alice Springs.

For those with more time, follow Larapinta Drive back to Alice Springs via Gosse Bluff Crater (Tnorala) and Hermannsburg → p. 87. To be able to cross Aboriginal territory, however, you need a Meerenie Tour Pass that is available in Alice Springs (Visitor Information Centre) or in Glen Helen Resort. Goose Bluff Crater was created 140 million years ago through the impact of a meteorite. Hermannsburg was the first missionary station set up by Lutherans in Northern Territory and was the home of the Aborigine artist Albert Namatjira (1902–59). Namatjira's watercolours have influenced the style of three generations of artists since then. The mission was built in 1877 and was only returned to its traditional owners, the Aranda, in 1982. Today, the station can be visited for a small fee and, while there, you should definitely try the apple strudel in the coffeeshop.

2 STEEP CLIFFS, ENDLESS BEACHES AND SECRET FORESTS

The Great Ocean Road south of Melbourne is one of the most beautiful stretches of coastline in the world. The 345km (215mi)-long road winds its way past endless beaches and

The huge Gosse Bluff Crater was created by a meteorite

The Great Ocean Road leads past Otway National Park

steep cliffs. The white-cap waves from the glittering turquiose ocean crash onto sandbanks or breath-taking rock formations. Those who don't intend just zooming past the superb natural scenery and the secrets hidden further inland, but also want to see things close up, should plan at least 3–4 days.

The ★ *Great Ocean Road (www.great oceanroad.com.au)* begins in the port Geelong (pop. 140,000), 70km (44mi) from Melbourne down the the M 1/Princes Freeway. The quayside of this former industrial port is now home to a number of restaurants. The long Eastern Beach ends at the botanic garden. Something special is the restored Art Deco saltwater pool in which swimmers are safe from sharks. The Great Ocean Road, that is signposted from Geelong, leads to Torquay (pop. 3500), a mekka for surf fans with INSIDERTIP specialist shops for surfers and even a surfing museum *(Surfworld | Surfcoast*

Plaza | Beach Road | Mon–Fri 9am–5pm, Sat/Sun 10am–4pm | A$8). At Easter, the international *Bell's Beach Surfing Classic* for professionals is held on legendary Bell's Beach, 2km (1¼mi) south of Torquay. The waves, up to 4m (13ft) high, are nothing for beginners. Carry on down the Great Ocean Road to the small resort of Anglesea and on to Lorne (pop. 1000), the tourist centre of the coastal road with a wonderful sandy beach and accommodation to suit every taste. *(Information: Lorne Visitors Centre | 144 Mountjoy Parade | tel. 03 52 89 11 52 | www. lornelink. com.au*

Apollo Bay → p. 65 45km (28mi) further south, is a quieter spot where you can unwind, go for a swim, fish and hike through the hinterland in the secretive INSIDERTIP *Otway National Park*. Very few foreign tourists find their way here: huge tree ferns and lofty eucalyptus trees provide shade along the narrow trails.

You have to climb over moss-covered jungle giants lying across the path and wade through crystal-clear streams, past sparkling waterfalls. During the day you will see cockatoos and birds of prey. At night, possums, owls and gliders – that look like flying squirrels – are out and about and thousands of glow-worms shine away among the mossy overhanging banks. This is also where you come to after a short walk at the end the interesting 3–4 hour 'Paddle with the Platypus' tour, organised by Otway Eco Tours *(approx. A$85 | tel. 03 52 36 63 45 | www.platypustours.net. au)*. Tours start in the late afternoon in the little village of Forrest. The probability of actually seeing platypuses is quite high. Great Ocean walks lasting one or several days and mountainbike tours are also on offer.

From Apollo Bay, head for Port Campbell (95km/59mi). After 17km (10½mi) through shady woods, a sign on the left points to Maits Rest. A boardwalk from the carpark takes you through an enchanting and unique 'niche' rainforest. The circuit takes 40 mins. A few miles further on, a narrow, 13km (8mi)-long road to the left of the Ocean Road, leads to the old ☼ Cape Otway Lighthouse on a 100m (328ft)-high bluff jutting out into the sea. The lighthouse *(daily 9.30am–4.30pm | A$9)* was built by convicts in 1848.

For the next 40km (25mi), the Great Ocean Road cuts through shady woods past small, hidden farms, to Port Campbell. From Princetown the road follows the cliffs through Port Campbell National Park. Breath-taking rock formations, shining brilliantly in the sun, rise above the deep-blue water: the Twelve Apostles. A first and good impression of these natural limestone statues formed by the sea (there are only actually seven still standing) can be had at ☼ Gibson Step Lookout. From here, steep steps lead down to the beach below the craggy cliffs. In good weather, you can walk along the beach from here to the first Apostles. Just a little bit further on, you turn right to the ☼ Twelve Apostles Lookout carpark, from where you have a spectacular view of the stacks, bridges and arches that make up the Twelve Apostles.

Driving on towards Port Campbell you pass Loch Ard Gorge. Port Campbell is a tiny fishing village with a pretty, safe beach and pleasant restaurants, e.g. *Waves (29 Lord Street)*, serving excellent fish with an Indian-Pacific touch *(tel. 03 55 98 6111 | open every day | Moderate)*.

From Port Campbell, the road continues to Warrnambool (pop. 22,500, *www. warrnamboolinfo.com.au*). This former

On the Great Ocean Road

Loch Ard Gorge is a perfect place to break your journey

whaling town is now a destination for whale-watchers. In the Australian winter, from June–September, the Southern Right Whales come here to calve in the bay, just a few yards off Logans Beach.

Chilly whale-watchers can warm up in the tearoom at Flagstaff Hill Maritime Museum *(Merri Street | daily 9am–5pm | A$7)*. The museum is a living village – a reproduction of a 19th-century port with shipbuilders, smiths, artists, a school, a little church, pub and bank. The evening sound and laser show, 'Shipwrecked', ensures the memory of this stretch of coastline's history with its tragic wrecks in upheld *(reservations tel. 03 55 59 46 00 | www.flagstaffhill.com)*.

From Warrnambool it is another 30km (19mi) to the small historical town of Port Fairy → p. 67. A detour to INSIDER TIP Tower Hill State Game Reserve, 12km (7½mi) west of Warrnambool is well worthwhile. Tower Hill is the deep crater of an extinct volcano. Within its rim, a fascinating wilderness has evolved in which kangaroos, koalas and thousands of birds are at home. Special care should be taken driving along this circular route, especially in the late afternoon and evening, as there are animals everywhere.

Sleepy Cape Bridgewater with its numerous coastal paths, black volcanic rock and primeval petrified forest can be reached via Portland (80km/50mi). From Warrnambool you can take the direct route back to Geelong along the A1, the Princes Highway, in the direction of Colac (approx. 215km/133mi).

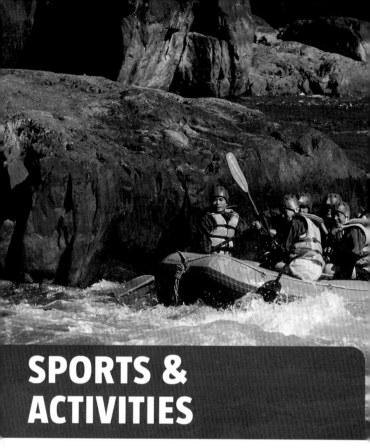

SPORTS & ACTIVITIES

You can swim, surf, sail and dive in many places around the virtually infinite coastline of this island continent. And in the mountains you can go climbing and even skiing. Extreme sports enthusiasts can find exactly what they are looking for here.

CANOEING & KAYAK RAFTING

Australia's lonely, long coastline and the untamed, clear rivers of Tasmania or the Snowy Mountains are ideal for sea kayaking, canoeing and rafting. There are many small businesses in the hundreds of coastal resorts or on the edge of national parks which have canoes, kayaks and equipment for hire or which organise guided tours. **INSIDER TIP** *World Expeditions (71 York Street | Sydney | tel. 02 82 70 84 00 | www. worldexpeditions.com.au)* offer tours lasting anything from one day to two weeks everywhere in Australia, often taking in visits to Aboriginal communities, e.g. the *Larapinta Trail,* 6 days, approx. A$2000, starting from Alice Springs.

DIVING

While the Barrier Reef is certainly the best-known destination for underwater sports fans *(www.divingqueensland.com)*, there

On the Australian continent, sport is combined with undiluted nature – and the possibilities are endless

are interesting dives to be had almost everywhere. The colourful Ningaloo Reef in Western Australia is becoming increasingly popular. Trial dives such as those available on the Barrier Reef are a good way of finding out a little bit more about one of the most fascinating sports there is. Under strict supervision and equipped with cylinders, flippers, goggles and a snorkel, even the nervously inclined can discover the undersea world for themselves up to a depth of 5m (16ft). After a 1-hour theory lesson, it's into the water. Attending a diving school course is definitely the cheapest way to dive in Australia. A 1-week foundation course costs approx. A$500.

Trial dives on the Great Barrier Reef are available through *Quicksilver (tel. 07 40 99 50 50)* in Port Douglas, for example. 3-day diving expeditions into the realm of the great white shark can be booked through *Rodney Fox* (from A$2500). The documentary film-maker and shark expert has a small museum at Victor Harbour in the Whale Centre *(www.rodneyfox.com.au).* More information on diving and the addresses of approved diving schools can be found under: *PADI (Professional Association of Diving Instructors) | www.padi.com.*

GOLF

Golf is played everywhere on the continent – even in the middle of the desert. Most golf clubs are open to non-members. Green fees for a round are between A$30–180. Clubs and sometimes even shoes can be hired for around A$40. Information: *Australian Golf Union | 153–155 Cecil Street | Melbourne | tel. 03 96 99 79 44 | www.agu.org.au*

HIKING

Well-marked hiking trails, refreshments and accommodation are generally only to be found near large urban centres or in tourist areas. If you want to go on hikes lasting several days in the huge national parks, you need to take your own camping gear, food and often your own water, and be able to use a compass and read a topographic map. Before you disappear into the bush, it is important you inform the appropriate ranger office of your planned route and expected time of return.

In many places you can rent a GPS system or an emergency beacon for a small fee, so that you can be found more easily in the middle of the wilderness. Well-known bush walks include the *Royal National Park Coastal Walk* near Sydney, the *Fraser Island Walk* in Queensland and the *Overland Track* in Tasmania. Those hiking in Australia for the first time should join an experienced group to start with, or book a guided tour.

A selection of tours can be found, for example, under *www.worldexpeditions.com.au.*

RIDING

You can ride almost anywhere in Australia: at riding schools, in parks and city suburbs, on huge cattle or sheep stations (hacks often being part of a stay-on-a-farm package), on beaches and through rainforests – or in a rider's absolute paradise, the Snowy Mountains **INSIDER TIP** *(Reynella Rides | Roslyn and John Rudd | Reynella | Adaminaby | tel. 02 64 54 23 86 | www. reynellarides.com.au | 3 days/4 nights A$1100 | 5 days/6 nights A$1700 | incl. horse, riding hat, tent and camping equipment, overnight stays on a farm and all meals).*

SAILING & SURFING

There are sailing schools and associations in all large Australian town on the coast

and in many resorts where you can either learn to sail or sail as a member of the crew. Information and pricelists can usually be found at local visitor information offices. Sailing in Sydney Harbour is fun even for those who are not fully seaworthy. *Sail Australia (Cremorne | Sydney | tel. 02 99 60 61 11 | www.sailaustralia.com.au)* organises harbour sailing trips. You can either sail on your own or with an experienced skipper, *prices from A$90 per person.* A great experience is also a cruise on a maxi yacht to the Whitsunday Islands, available for example through *Barefoot Cruises Australia (from Airley Beach | tel. 07 49 46 17 77 | www.barefootcruises.com.au | from A$320 for 2 days/1 night).*

Surf schools can be found on most patrolled beaches in Australia. *Sydney Safe Surf Schools (The Pavillion, Marine Parade | tel. 02 93 65 43 70 | www.safesurfschools. com.au)* on the beach in Maroubra offers INSIDER TIP excellent introductory courses

away from all the tourists for A$55 for 2 hours, incl. surfboard and wetsuit. *Surf & Stay* is provided by *Mojo Surf* on the eastern side of Byron Bay: e.g. 4 days incl. full board, equipment and instruction for A$450 *(tel. 02 66 39 51 00 or 1800 11 30 44 | www.mojosurf.com).* Surfies congregate on beaches along the Great Ocean Road, especially on Bell's Beach, on the Gold Coast, where Surfers' Paradise promises just that on earth, or on the west coast in the south, infamous for its crashing breakers and therefore only for experienced surfers. For more on the top spots, see: *www.surfing-waves.com,* or *www.surfing australia.com.* Windsurfers swear by the west coast of the continent, the area around Perth being ideal – even for beginners, who can find a windsurfing school at Pelican Point on the north bank of the Swan River where kitesurfing is also available *(Windforce Watersports | tel. 08 93 86 18 30 | www.windforce.com.au).*

Hiking in Australia's national parks can be a real adventure

TRAVEL WITH KIDS

Australia is a very child-friendly country. Hotels, museums and leisure parks, buses, trains and ferries often have considerably reduced family rates. Many useful tips can be found under *www.holidayswithkids.com.au.*

ADVENTUREWORLD (170 B5) *(* B6)
Mysterious caves, a castle lookout, a chair lift and any number of pools to splash around in. *79 Progress DriveBibra Lake | 16km (10mi) south of Perth | www.adventureworld.net.au | Oct–April daily 10am–5pm | adults A$49, children A$41*

ALPENRAIL (179 D6) *(* H8)
This huge model railway chugs around a 200m² Swiss mountain landscape across lots of bridges and past houses and over roads. *82 Abbotsfield Road | Claremont near Hobart | www.alpenrail.com.au | daily April–Sept. 10am–4.30pm, Oct–March 9.30am–4.30pm | adults A$13, children A$7*

BALMORAL BEACH (177 E6) *(* J6)
If the powerful waves on the east coast are too dangerous for your children and you still fancy a swim on one of Sydney's beach-es, then Balmoral is the ideal place for you. This sheltered bay is to the north of the pretty suburb's harbour. While the children build sandcastles parents can have a tasty lunch in the *Bathers' Pavilion* and enjoy the view. *Tel. 02 99 69 50 50 | www.batherspavilion.com.au | lunch and dinner daily, Sundays breakfast too | Expensive*

COLLINGWOOD CHILDREN'S FARM (179 D2) *(* G7)
A hands-on farm where the goats and sheep can be stroked. Pony rides available. The cows are milked at 10am and 4pm. *Daily 9am–5pm | 18 St Heliers St. | Abbotsford, in northeast Melbourne | tel. 03 94 17 58 06 | A$16 per family*

HAIGH'S CHOCOLATES VISITORS CENTRE (175 D6) *(* F6)
Watch chocolate being made, try some yourself – and buy a few treats for the road. Guided tours through the factory located in the south of Adelaide are free of charge and a real temptation for the sweet-toothed of all ages. *154 Greenhill Rd. | Parkside | www.haighschocolates.com | Mon–Fri 8.30am–5.30pm, Sat 9am–5pm*

A continent for kids – there are great parks, steam trains and lots of adventures to be had down under

GOLD COAST THEME PARKS
(177 F1) (𝒸 J5)

Fun, fun, fun: approx. 60km (37mi) south of Brisbane and a 20-minute drive to the north from Surfers Paradise (Gold Coast), fun is the name of the game: *Seaworld* (www.seaworld.com.au) with dolphin shows and water acrobatics, the great Warner Bros. film park *Movieworld* (www. movieworld.com.au) and, right next door, the *Wet 'n' Wild* water theme park and the *Australian Outback Spectacular* (www.out backspectacular.com.au) that is really more for adults. *Dreamworld* (www.dreamworld. com.au) is a theme park with a variety of rides incl. a rollercoaster. *Daily 10am–5pm | adults from A$64, children from A$42*

PUFFING BILLY (179 D2) (𝒸 G7)

2-hour round trip on the oldest steam train still running in Australia. *40km (25mi) east of Melbourne | Old Monbulk Road |* *Belgrave Station | www.puffingbilly.com. au | adults from A$25, children from A$12*

QUESTACON (177 D6) (𝒸 H7)

The National Science & Technology Centre in Canberra boasts more than 170 interactive displays. *King Edward Terrace | www. questacon.edu.au | daily 9am–5pm | adults A$20, children A$15*

INSIDER TIP ▶ SPECTACULAR JUMPING CROCODILE CRUISE (158 C2) (𝒸 E1)

This boat trip on the Adelaide River tempts saltwater crocodiles to leap out of the water, snapping at meat dangled over the railing. An unforgettable experience for children who otherwise only know motionless crocs in zoos. *Arnhem Highway | on the road to Kakadu National Park (turning off to 'Window of the Wetlands' viewpoint) | www.jumpingcrocodile.com.au | daily 9am, 11am, 1pm, 3pm | A$70 per family*

FESTIVALS & EVENTS

As the weather is generally pretty reliable, everything takes place in the great outdoors. Whether a sporting challenge or a cultural treat, the most important thing is that everyone has a good time – and visitors are always welcome.

PUBLIC HOLIDAYS

1 Jan *New Year's Day*; **26 Jan** *Australia Day*; Good Friday, Easter Monday; **25 April** *Anzac Day*; **2nd Mon** in June *Queen's Birthday*; **25/26 Dec** *Christmas*

REGIONAL FESTIVALS

JANUARY

During the 3-week ▶ *Sydney Festival* there are any number of exhibitions, plays, dance performances, music events and street art *(www.sydneyfestival.org.au)*.

FEBRUARY

▶ *Gay and Lesbian Mardi Gras* in Sydney: a 1-month-long festival for locals and visitors from all over the world, culminating in a huge parade and party *(www.mardigras.org.au)*.

The almost 4-week-long ▶ *Festival of Perth* is the oldest cultural festival in Australia, well known for good and innovative theatrical performances *(www.perthfestival.com.au)*.

MARCH

▶ *Moomba Festival* in Melbourne: large carnival procession and many cultural events *(www.melbourne.vic.gov.au)*.

APRIL

▶ *Rip Curl Pro:* International surfing competition at Bell's Beach in Victoria *(www.bellsbeachaustralia.com)*.

MAY

You can watch herdsmen test their skills at the ▶ INSIDER TIP ▶ *Outback Muster Reunion* in the Stockman's Hall of Fame in Longreach. For 3 days everything revolves around cattle and sheep minding *(www.destinationlongreach.com.au)*.

JUNE

The ▶ *Mowanjum Festival* in Derby in Kimberley is a showcase for Aboriginal artists *(www.derbytourism.com.au)*.

Most Australian events take place outside –
a highlight in the calendar is definitely the
Melbourne Cup

JULY

On the 2nd Sat in the month, countless camels line up at the start of the ▶ *Lion's Camel Cup* race in Alice Springs *(www.camelcup.com.au)*.

AUGUST

The ▶ *Henley on Todd Regatta* in Alice Springs in the dried up Todd River is certainly the weirdest 'regatta' in the world *(www.henleyontodd.com.au)* and, at the ▶ *Darwin Beer Can Regatta,* only craft made of empty cans are permitted to take part *(www.beercanregatta.org.au)*. The ▶ INSIDER TIP *Isa Rodeo* in the mining town of Mount Isa in Queensland is where you'll find wild bulls, bucking broncos, real men and pretty cowgirls *(www.isarodeo.com.au)*. The ▶ *Festival of the Pearl* in the former pearl capital Broome is one of the most important and colourful festivals in Australia *(www.shinjumatsuri.com.au)*.

SEPTEMBER

Artists from all ethnic groups come together at the ▶ *Festival of Darwin (www.darwinfestival.org.au)*.
For many Melbournians, the ▶ *AFL*, the ▶ *Australian Football Grand Finale* in Melbourne, is the most important event in the year *(www.afl.com.au)*.

OCTOBER

The multicultural ▶ *Melbourne (Art) Festival* starts off with a procession from Brunswick Street *(www.melbournefestival.com.au)*.

NOVEMBER

The whole nation comes to a grinding halt for the ▶ ★ *Melbourne Cup* horse race that takes place every year on the 1st Tuesday in November. In Victoria, it is a public holiday *(www.melbournecup.com)*.

LINKS, BLOGS, APPS & MORE

LINKS

▶ www.australia.com/about.aspx All sorts of information covering the whole continent at a glance to help you plan a holiday down under. Includes information about the culture and history, food and wine, artworks and magnificent natural landscape

▶ www.exploroz.com Excellent tips for all those who want to explore things off the beaten track and want to find some good suggested routes

▶ www.ga.gov.au Indispensable for anyone who wants to take a closer look at the geography of Australia (Geoscience Australia) and with a penchant for maps

▶ www.aboriginalaustralia.com.au List of various tours that guarantee an excellent insight into the culture of the Aborigines

▶ www.pandora.nla.gov.au Australia's web archive. Everything online that is of economic, scientific or cultural relevance for the country is copied and stored here

▶ www.australianexplorer.com Detailed and well-structured page with tourist-related information covering all states, incl. tours on offer and accommodation

▶ www.walkaboutplanner.australia.com The most beautiful car trips throughout the continent; with clear and detailed descriptions

▶ www.agfg.com.au The 'Australian Good Food and Travel Guide' is logically structured and very up-to-date with the best restaurants and cafés

▶ www.wotflight.com An overview of domestic (inland) flights on offer and cheap tickets

Regardless of whether you are still preparing your trip or already in Australia: these addresses will provide you with more information, videos and networks to make your holiday even more enjoyable

BLOGS

▶ www.australiablog.com Bursting with information and blogs on all sorts of useful things

▶ www.expat-blog.com/en/directory/oceania/australia Living and working in Australia written by ex-pats keen to share their first-hand experience

▶ www.travelblog.org/Oceania/Australia Thousands of travel blogs covering all regions of Australia

▶ http://blogpond.com.au With the 100 most popular Australian blogs (and much more too)

VIDEOS

▶ www.sbs.com.au Countless interesting podcasts as well as news and other items provided by the multicultural and multilingual SBS broadcasting company

▶ www.youtube.com/australiasoutback Various videos downloaded by Tourism Northern Territory. If you search under Youtube Australia a whole array of other videos is listed covering other areas of the continent

APPS

▶ Experience WA 7000 points of interest to tourists in Western Australia are available free of charge for iPhone, iPad and Android smartphones and tablets

▶ The Australian Android app News, analyses and commentaries on politics, media, health and anything that is of general interest

NETWORK

▶ www.tripbod.com This is where you can get to know the locals who take visitors by the hand and act as live travel guides – for a small fee, that is. Just enter 'Australia' in the search function. Things are still in the early stages

▶ www.digsville.com If you fancy doing a house swap with someone in Australia, then this is the right place. Alternatives (albeit not cheap) can be found under www.airbnb.com. For those who are not particularly choosy, try www.couchsurfing.com or www.homestayweb.com

TRAVEL TIPS

ARRIVAL

Flights from London to the east coast of Australia take 23+ hours. The long journey is more pleasant if you stop over in Singapore or Hong Kong, for example. Depending on the day, the time of year and the carrier, an economy class return ticket from London can cost anything from around £900/US$1400 upwards. It is worth not just comparing prices but also checking whether taxes and other fees are included. Some airlines such as Qantas *(www.qantas.com.au)* and Cathay Pacific *(www.cathaypacific.com)* offer cheap or even free tickets for domestic flights within Australia when you purchase an international ticket.

BANKS & MONEY

Money can be changed, cash obtained from dispensers with bank and credit cards, and travellers checks cashed without any problem at banks in major cities and tourist centres (opening times generally Mon–Fri 9am–4pm). Credit cards (especially Visa and Mastercard) are widely accepted. In the outback, payment by cash is still the norm, so make sure you carry enough cash with you.

CAR HIRE

Hiring a car in Australia is comparatively cheap, as is diesel and petrol (A$1.45–A$1.70/litre). Whether you need a 4-wheel-drive or not obviously depends on the route you're planning. Make sure your car hire company permits off-road driving (on unsurfaced/gravel roads) and take out a fully comprehensive insurance without co-payment. Be careful about supplements such as if you drop the car in a different city or extra charges for credit card payments. An international driving licence is obligatory. The best offers for campervans can be found online. Major hire companies include *www.maui.com.au, www.apollo camper.com* and *www.keacampers.com.*

CLIMATE, WHEN TO GO

The southeast (New South Wales, Tasmania, Victoria and South Australia) as well as Western Australia south of the Tropic of Capricorn, are best visited between Oct and April; Queensland, Northern Territory and the north of Western Australia between April and November. At other times of the year it is generally cool in the south, and hot and sticky in the north (north of the Tropic of Capricorn) – and it can rain very heavily. During the summer holidays in December and January, campsites near the coast are generally fully booked.

RESPONSIBLE TRAVEL

It doesn't take a lot to be environmentally friendly whilst travelling. Don't just think about your carbon footprint whilst flying to and from your holiday destination but also about how you can protect nature and culture abroad. As a tourist it is especially important to respect nature, look out for local products, cycle instead of driving, save water and much more. If you would like to find out more about eco-tourism please visit: *www.ecotourism.org*

From arrival to weather

Holiday from start to finish: the most important addresses and information for your trip to Australia

CONSULATES & EMBASSIES

BRITISH HIGH COMMISSION
Commonwealth Avenue | Canberra | ACT 2600 | tel. +612 62 70 66 66 (general enquiries) | ukinaustralia.fco.gov.uk

Apart from the High Commission, the United Kingdom has nine other offices in Australia, including the British Consulate in Sydney:

BRITISH CONSULATE-GENERAL
Level 16, Gateway Building | 1 Macquarie Place | Sydney |NSW 2000 | tel. +612 92 47 75 21 | ukinaustralia.fco.gov.uk/en
For more information see: *ukinaustralia. fco.gov.uk/en/about-us/other-locations/*

EMBASSY OF THE UNITED STATES OF AMERICA
Moonah Place | Yarralumla | Canberra | ACT 2600 | tel. +612 62 14 56 00 | canberra. usembassy.gov/contact.html

CUSTOMS

As a precaution against possible infection, no fruit, vegetables or meat may be taken into Australia. You may take 250 cigarettes, 250g tobacco and 2¼ litres of alcohol with you as well as personal items such as presents up to a value of A$900. For purchases of more than A$300 in a shop in Australia you can reclaim the 10% VAT at the airport when you depart. You must however show the items purchased at customs *(www.customs.gov.au)*. On returning to the EU, you may bring in 200 cigarettes or 50 cigars or 250g tobacco, 1 L of spirits or 4L wine, 250g coffee and other good up to a value of £340/€430. Travellers to the US who are residents of the country do not have to pay duty on articles purchased overseas up to the value of $800, but there are limits on the amount of alcoholic beverages and tobacco products. For the regulations for international travel for US residents please see *www.cbp.gov*

BUDGETING

Coffee	£2.40/$3.80	*for a latte macchiato in a restaurant*
Beer	£2.80/$4.50	*for a pint in a pub*
Wine	£4/$6.50	*for a glass of wine*
Pie	£2/$3.30	*for pub food*
Petrol	£1/$1.60	*for 1 litre*
Bus ticket	£1.60/$2.50	*for a standard journey*

DRIVING

The Australians drive on the left and give way to traffic coming from the right. Vehicles entering a roundabout have right of way. In general, the speed limit in a built-up area is 30 or 40mph, outside towns 60mph, and 70mph on motorways (80mph in Northern Territory). True motorways can only be found near major cities. Many so-called highways are two-way country roads with occassional overtaking lanes.

ELECTRICITY

240 Volts/AC. Most standard European devices operate without any problem but you do need an adapter, available for example at airports, luggage shops or chemists.

EMMERGENCY SERVICES

Tel. 000, callers must then say if they want the fire, police or ambulance.

HEALTH

UK and Irish citizens, and those from several other European nations, are entitled to free reciprocal Medicare treatment in Australian hospitals and at GPs, although there are certain restrictions. It is best to familiarise yourself beforehand of the conditions of the reciprocal arrangement as these do not, for example, cover private hospitals which can be very expensive. It is worth looking into the cost of an additional health insurance before your journey.

IMMIGRATION

A tourist visa is need to enter Australia (does not apply to New Zealanders) that can usually be issued or applied for when purchasing a plane ticket (eVisitor visa). It is valid for a stay of up to 3 months. It is strictly forbidden to take paid employment of any kind and failing to observe this law could result in a heavy fine. People between 18–30 years of age may apply for a special work-and-travel visa valid for up to 2 years which allows them to accept temporary employment *(www.immi.gov.au)*.

INFORMATION

Australian tourist or visitor information offices can be found in all major cities and tourist centres and provide maps, travel guides and general information. See: *www.australia.com*

BOOKS & FILMS

▶ **Remembering Babylon** – by David Malouf. European settlers in the north of Australia come face to face with an unfamiliar environment and the Aborigines. A plea for tolerance and understanding between cultures.

▶ **The Fatal Shore. The epic of Australia's founding** – by Robert Hughes. Impressive historical account of the pain and suffering endured during the first decades of the penal colony.

▶ **Priscilla – Queen of the Desert** – directed by Stephan Elliott. Cult film about the weird and wonderful adventures three drag queens have after setting out in a clapped-out bus called Priscilla, on their 3000km (1900mi) journey to Alice Springs where they are scheduled to perform. With music from Abba. The musical 'Priscilla' has been running in Melbourne since 2006.

▶ **Australia** – directed by Baz Luhrmann. At the end of 2008, Australia's biggest film production to date hit the cinemas. A romantic outback epic starring Nicole Kidman and Hugh Jackman.

'Animals on road'

INLAND FLIGHTS

If there are no domestic flights included with your international air ticket, flights can easily be booked on the Internet and paid for by credit card. You will then receive an e-ticket and only have to show your passport when checking in. Competition among budget airlines is huge: *Jetstar (www.jet star.com)*, *Virgin Australia (www.virginaus tralia.com)*, *Tiger Airways (www.tigerair ways.com)*. Prices for inland flights vary considerably. The earlier you book, the better. In the southeast, *Regional Express (www. rex.com.au)* also flies to remote regions.

INTERNET

Information about most aspects of a trip to Australia can usually be found online. Public transport is listed under *www.bus lines.com.au. www.communityguide.com. au* is rather like the Yellow Pages and logically structured. Information on resources and publications in Australia can be found under *www.archivists.org.au.* A perfect weather service is available through *www. bom.gov.au.* The *Charles Sturt University* website for tourists to Australia is very informative: *www.csu.edu.au/australia.*

INTERNET CAFÉS & WI-FI

The infrastructure in Australia is good, especially in towns, with Internet cafés virtually on every street corner. Local libraries often have cheap Internet rates. Free Wi-Fi can generally only be found in larger centres, but is also available on a number of campsites. A list of some 2500 free or commercial hotspots can be found under: *www.jiwire.com.*

OPENING HOURS

Restaurants, pubs, food shops and information offices in the larger towns are generally open every day. In rural areas, most things are closed at weekends. In the outback, petrol stations, motels and small restaurants often shut at 6pm.

PHONE & MOBILE PHONE

The international dialling code for Australia is *61*, followed by the area code without the *0*, i.e. *2* for Sydney. From Australia, the dialling code is *0011 +44* for the UK, *0011 +1* for the USA and Canada. Toll-free numbers start with *1800*; 6-digit numbers that start with *13* are charged as local calls. In many telephone boxes you can only call with a telephone card that is available from news agencies and post offices.

Prepaid cards for mobile phones for use in Australia can be bought before your journey for a set fee which normally includes a number of free calls. You will then have a new number and can take incoming calls free of charge. The best network in Australia (also for surfing) is *Telstra (www.telstra.com.au)*. You can also transfer data from your own USB stick with, for example, the *Telstra Pre-Paid Mobile Wi-Fi* (for A$130: 5GB for 90 days). Satellite telephones are an alternative for use in the outback. These can also be rented, prepaid *(e.g. www.trtelecom. com)*.

POST

Even the tiniest village has a post office. A postcard to Europe costs A$1.60, a letter A$2.35 and takes about 6 days. For more information see: *www.auspost.com.au*

PRICES & CURRENCY

The unit of currency is the Australian dollar (A$). There are 10, 20, 50 and 100 Aus-

WEATHER IN SYDNEY

	Jan	Feb	March	April	May	June	July	Aug	Sept	Oct	Nov	Dec
Daytime temperatures in °C/°F	26/79	26/79	24/75	22/72	19/66	16/61	16/61	17/63	19/66	22/72	23/73	25/77
Nighttime temperatures in °C/°F	18/64	18/64	17/63	14/57	11/52	9/48	8/46	9/48	11/52	13/55	16/61	17/63
Sunshine hours/day	7	7	6	5	5	4	5	6	6	7	7	7
Precipitation days/month	7	8	8	7	5	9	5	7	7	9	8	8
Water temperatures in °C/°F	23/73	24/75	23/73	20/68	18/64	18/64	16/61	17/63	18/64	19/66	19/66	21/70

tralian dollar notes, 1 and 2 dollar coins and 5, 10, 20 and 50 cent coins. Prices for goods and services are comparable to those in Britain. Some food is slightly more expensive.

TIME

There are 3 time zones in Australia. In Western Australia: Western Standard Time (GMT +8 hours), in Northern Territory and in South Australia: Central Standard Time (GMT +9½ hours), in the other states: Eastern Standard Time (GMT +10 hours). In most states (except Queensland, Northern Territory and Western Australia) summer time is between the 1st Sun in Oct and the 1st Sun in April.

TRAINS & BUSES

Australia can easily be explored by train or bus. It is often a good idea to buy bus passes for overland journeys before starting your journey. Such passes either allow you to make an unlimited number of stops on any chosen route, are divided into categories according to distance or give you a reduction of 50%. The market is dominated by *Greyhound (tel.* +61 7 32 58 16 00 | www.greyhound.com.au)*. Due to the restricted capacity on trains you should always check availability beforehand *(www. railaustralia.com.au)*. For more information see: *www.greyhound.com.au* and *www. railaustralia.com.au/flexipass.php*

WHERE TO STAY, CAMPING

Hotels in major cities are expensive (A$140–280 for 3–4 star hotels), flats and apartments are often a better alternative. They are bigger, better equipped and slightly cheaper. There are also a lot of holiday homes for rent *(www.stayz.com.*

au). Outside urban centres there are lots of motels (A$90–150). Campsites *(www. goseeaustralia.com.au, www.campsaustra liawide.com.au, also lists free sites)* often have cabins and motel rooms (A$50–120).

CURRENCY CONVERTER

£	A$	A$	£
1	1.60	1	0.65
3	4.80	3	1.90
5	8	5	3.15
13	21	13	8.20
40	64	40	25
75	120	75	47
120	190	120	75
250	398	250	157
500	795	500	314

At the time of going to press, US$1 ≈ A$1.
For current exchange rates see www.xe.com

B&B is popular *(www.australianbedand breakfast.com.au)*, as is a stay on a station, as farms in Australia are called *(www. australiafarmstays.com.au, www.austral ianfarmtourism.com.au, www.farmstay holidays.com.au)*. Good accommodation can be found at short notice under *www. wotif.com.au* and *www.ratestogo.com.au*. There are lots of youth hostels and backpacker hostels which also have cheap double rooms. Rooms/houses available privately can be found under *www.airbnb. com, www.homestayweb.com* and *www. couchsurfing.org*.

For camping organisations in Australia (with campsite tips): NSW: *www.caravan-camping.com.au;* WA: *www.caravanwa. com.au;* QLD: *www.caravanqld.com.au;* SA: *www.sa-parks.com.au;* VIC: *www.vic-parks.com.au;* NT: *www.ntcaravanpark. com.au*

NOTES

MARCO POLO TRAVEL GUIDES

- PACKED WITH INSIDER TIPS
- BEST WALKS AND TOURS
- FULL-COLOUR PULL-OUT MAP
  AND STREET ATLAS

ROAD ATLAS

The green line ▬▬ indicates the Trips & Tours (p. 130–135)
The blue line ▬▬ indicates The perfect route (p. 30–31)

All tours are also marked on the pull-out map

Photo: Yellow Water Wetlands in Kakadu National Park

Exploring Australia

The map on the back cover shows how the area has been sub-divided

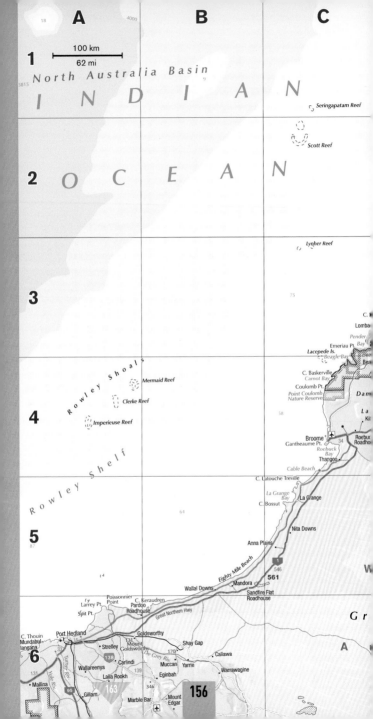

A   **B**   **C**

1

100 km
62 mi

North Australia Basin

I N D I A N

Seringapatam Reef

2

O C E A N

Scott Reef

3

Lynher Reef

C.
Lomba
Pender Bay
Emeriau Pt.
Lacepede Is.
Beagle Bay
Bea

4

Rowley Shoals

Mermaid Reef

Clerke Reef

Imperieuse Reef

C. Baskerville
Carnot Bay
Coulomb Pt.
Point Coulomb
Nature Reserve

Dam

L a
Kil

Rowley Shelf

Broome
Gantheaume Pt.
Roebuck
Roadho
Roebuck
Bay
Thangoo
Cable Beach

5

Rowley Shelf

C. Latouche Treville
La Grange
Bay
C. Bossut
La Grange

Nita Downs

Anna Plains

W

Eighty Mile Beach
546
561

Wallal Downs
Mandora
Sandfire Flat
Roadhouse

6

Larrey Pt.
Poissonnier
Point
C. Keraudren
Pardoo
Roadhouse
Spit Pt.
Great Northern Hwy

G r

C. Thouin
Mundabul-
langana
Port Hedland
Goldsworthy
Strelley
Mount
Goldsworthy
Shay Gap
Caliawa
A

Wallareenya
Carlindi
De Grey Riv.
Muccan
Yarrie
Warrawagine

163
Lalla Rookh
Gillam
95
138
170
139
346
Eginbah
156

Mallina
Marble Bar
Mount
Edgar

131

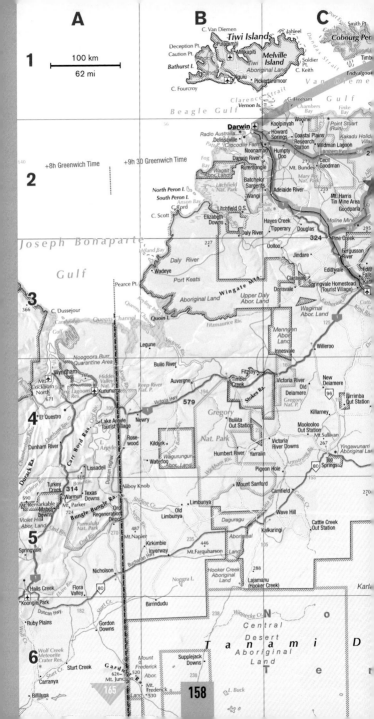

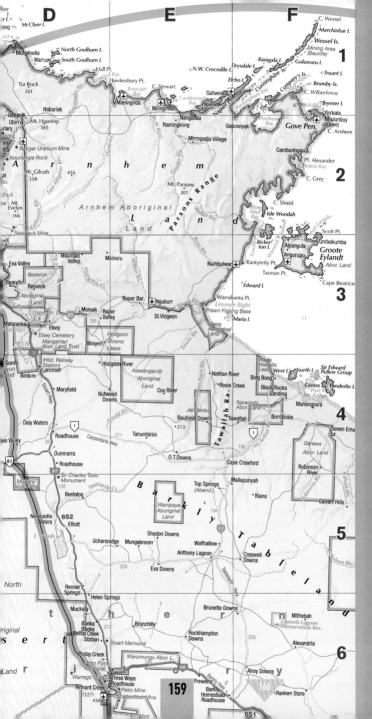

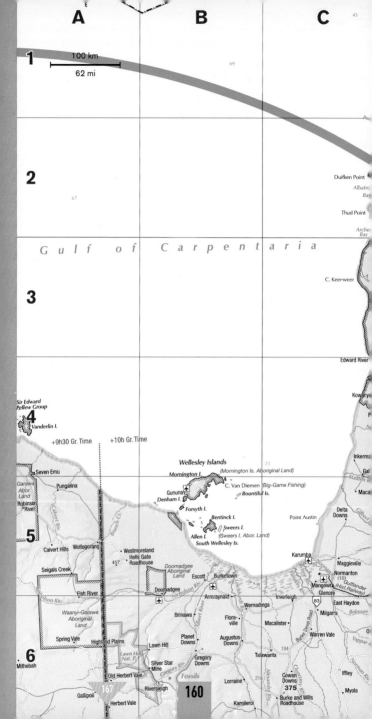

A

1 100 km
62 mi

69

B

C

45

67

2

Duifken Point

Albatross
Bay

Thud Point

Arche
Bay

G u l f   o f   C a r p e n t a r i a

C. Keer-weer

3

Edward River

Kowanya

Sir Edward
Pellew Group

4

Vanderlin I.

+9h30 Gr. Time   +10h Gr. Time

Inkerma

Wellesley Islands

23

Gal

Seven Emu

Mornington I.   (Mornington Is. Aboriginal Land)

Staaten

Garawa
Abor.
Land

Pungalina

Gununa
Denham I.

C. Van Diemen *(Big-Game Fishing)*

Maca

Bountiful Is.

Robinson
River

Forsyth I.

Bentinck I.

Delta
Downs

5

Sweers I.

Point Austin

Branch Cr.

Allen I. (Sweers I. Abor. Land)
South Wellesley Is.

Calvert Hills

Wollogorang

Calvert Riv.

Westmoreland
Hells Gate
Roadhouse

457

Karumba

Maggieville

Seigals Creek

*Doomadgee
Aboriginal
Land*

Escott

Burketown

Normanton
(10)

Gulflander
(Hist. Railway)

Fish River

Doomadgee

Armraynald

Inverleigh

Mangowra
Glenore

East Haydon

Nicholson Riv.

Brinawa

Wernadinga

83

Milgarra

Belmore

Waanyi-Garawa
Aboriginal
Land

Albert River

Flora-
ville

Macalister

Burke Devil Road

Warren Vale

Yappar

Spring Vale

Highland Plains

Planet
Downs

Augustus
Downs

Talawanta

194

6

Mithebah

Lawn Hill
Nat. P.

Lawn Hill

Silver Star
Mine

Gregory
Downs

Fossils

Cowan
Downs

218

Iffley

Myola

167

Old Herbert Vale

Riversleigh

160

Lorraine

Burke and Wills
Roadhouse

Norman Riv.

Galipoli

Herbert Vale

Kamileroi

Gregory Riv.

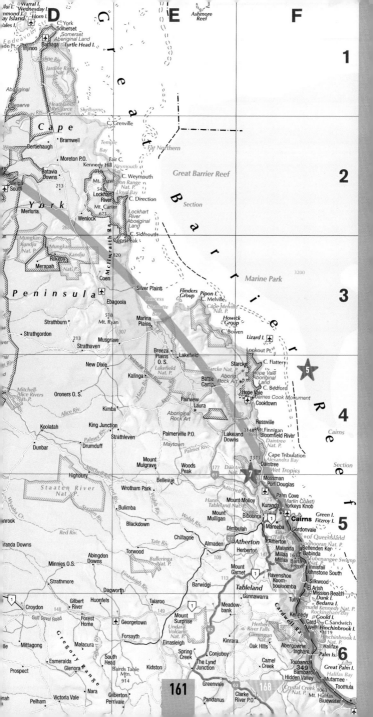

Warral I.
Wednesday I.
mond I.
ay Island
ales I.

Horn I.

York
Somerset
Aboriginal Land
Turtle Head I.

Barnaga

Injinoo

de Pt.

Endeavour

Jardine River
Nat. P.

Aboriginal
Reserve

Heathlands
Resource
Reserve

Bertiehaugh

C a p e

Bramwell

Moreton P.O.

Kennedy Hill

Fair C.

Temple
Bay

Batavia
Downs

Weipa
South

213

Mt. Tozer

Iron Range
Nat. P.

Lockhart
River

542

Weymouth
Bay

C. Weymouth

Lloyd Bay

Far Northern

C. Grenville

Shelburne
Bay

Great Barrier Reef
Section

Y o r k

Merluna

Mt. Carter

C. Direction

Wenlock

500 C. Sidmouth

Lockhart
River
Aboriginal
Land

Pefis Peak

820

B
a
r
r
i
e
r

Munkgan
Kandju
Nat. P.

Rokeby

Munkgan
Kandju
Nat. P.

3200

Merapah

Marine Park

P e n i n s u l a

Coen

Silver Plains

518

Strathburn

Ebagoola

Mt. Ryan

Princess
Charlotte

Flinders
Group

Pipon I.

Cape Melville
Nat. P.

Howick
Group

Strathgordon

213

Musgrave

307

Marina
Plains

C. Bowen

Strathaven

New Dixie

Breeza
Plains
O.S.

Lakefield

Lizard I.

Lookout Pt.

R
e
e
f

Mitchell-
Alice Rivers
Nat. P.

Kalinga

Lakefield
Nat. P.

Starcke

C. Flattery

Starcke Nat. P.

Oroners O.S.

Battle
Camp

Aborig.
Rock Art

Hope Vale
Aboriginal
Land

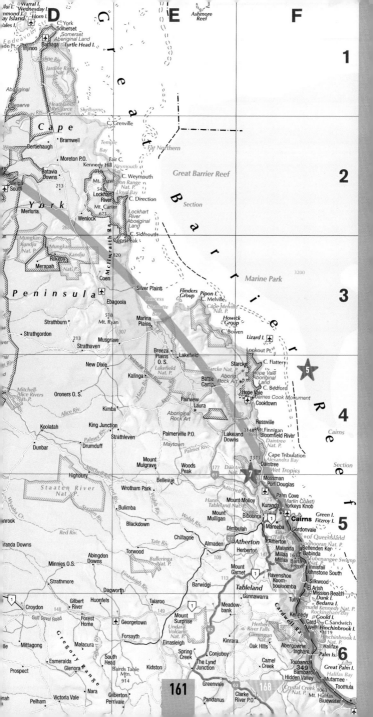

Dunbar

Kimba

Fairview

Laura

C. Bedford

James Cook Monument

Koolatah

King Junction

Strathleven

Aboriginal
Rock Art

Cooktown

Cairns
Section

Palmerville P.O.

Lakeland
Downs

Rossville

Dumbar

Palmer Riv.

1148 Mt. Finnigan

Bloomfield River

Drumduff

Highbury

Mount
Mulgrave

Maytown

Palmer Riv.

177

Daintree
Nat. P.

Alexandra Bay

Cape Tribulation

Woods
Peak

1375

Wet Tropics

Staaten River
Nat. P.

Bellevue

Mitchell Riv.

Daintree

81

Mossman

Wrotham Park

Hann
Tableland Nat. P.

Mount Molloy

Port Douglas

Palm Cove
(Martin Coast)

Bulimba

Mount
Mulligan

75

Kuranda

Yorkeys Knob

Blackdown

Chillagoe

Dimbulah

Biboohra

Cairns

Green I.
Fitzroy I.

Red Riv.

Almaden

Atherton

Mareeba

Gordonvale

Tate Riv.

Herberton

Malanda

Bellenden Ker

Babinda

Abingdon
Downs

Torwood

Bullerinya
Nat. P.

109

Mount
Garnet

Millaa
Millaa

1611

Wooroonooran Nat. P.

Bartle
Frere

Innisfail

Johnstone South

Minnies O.S.

Ravenshoe
Koom-
booloomba

113

Silkwood

El Arish

Strathmore

Dagworth

Barwidgi

Tableland

Gunnawarra

Mission Beach

Dunk I.

Bedarra I.

Croydon

Gilbert
River

148

Huonfels

Taiaroo

149

Meadow-
bank

Tully

Kennedy

Goold I.

Rockingham Bay

Forest
Home

Georgetown

Mount
Surprise

Undara
Volcanic
Nat. P.

Kinrara

Herbert
River Falls
Girringun
Nat. P.

Abergowrie

Inghamn

C. Sandwich

Hinchinbrook I.
Nat. P.

Palm Is.

Mittagong

Esmeralda

Malacura

Forsayth

62

Einasleigh

Spring
Creek

Conjuboy

Oak Hills

Camel
Creek

Toobanna

349

Great Palm I.

Mutarnee

Toomulla

Prospect

Glenora

South
Head

Bairds Table
Mtn.
914

Kidston

The Lynd
Junction

63

Clarke
River P.O.

Hidden Valley

Crystal Creek
Nat. P.

Mt. Halifax
Bluewater

1063

Halifax Bay

Victoria Vale

Nara

Gilberton

Greenvale

Pandanus

Pelham

Perrivale

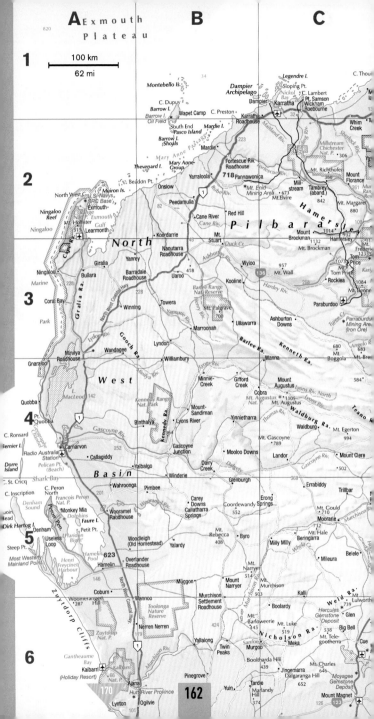

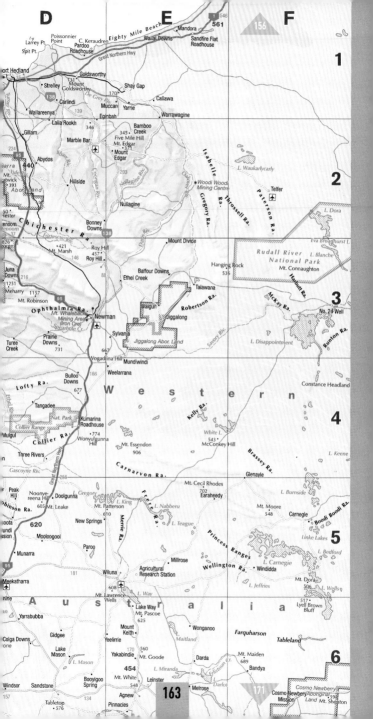

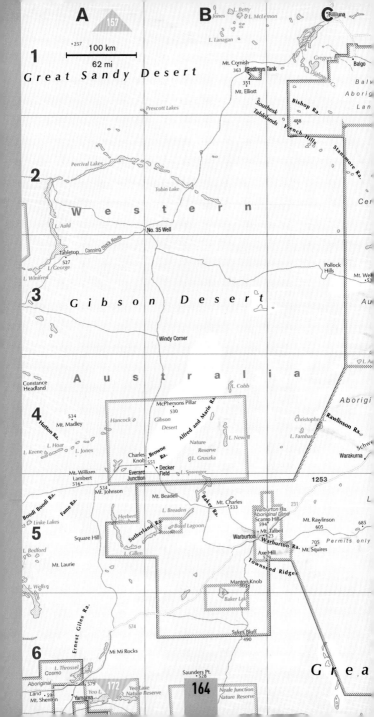

157

•257

100 km

62 mi

L. Betty

Jones • L. McLernon

L. Lanagan

Billiluna

Gregory • Balgo

Balgo

1

Great Sandy Desert

Mt. Cornish
363

Godfreys Tank
351

Mt. Elliott

Prescott Lakes

Southesk
Tablelands

Bishop Ra.

Balw
Aborig
Lan

French Hills
488

Stansmore Ra.

2

W e s t e r n

Percival Lakes

Tobin Lake

L. Auld

No. 35 Well

Canning Stock Route

Tabletop
527
L. George

L. Winifred

Pollock
Hills

Mt. We
•53

Cer

3

G i b s o n   D e s e r t

Windy Corner

Au

Constance
Headland

A u s t r a l i a

L. Cobb

Aborigi

4

Mt. Madley
534

Hancock

McPhersons Pillar
530

*Gibson
Desert*

Alfred and Marie Ra.

Rawlinson Ra.

Christophe

Hutton Ra.

L. Hoar

L. Keene L. Jones

Charles
Knob
551

Browne

Decker
Field

*Nature
Reserve*

L. Gruszka

L. Newell

L. Farnhan

Schw

Warakurna

Mt. William
Lambert
516

Everard
Junction

L. Sprenger

1253

5

Boodi Boodi Ra.

Fame Ra.

534
Mt. Johnson

Mt. Beadell

Baker Ra.

Mt. Charles
533

Warburton Ra.
Aboriginal Land
Scamp Hill
594

Mt. Rawlinson
605

685

L

L. Bedford

Linke Lakes

Square Hill

Herbert

L. Breaden

Budd Lagoon

Mt. Talbot
623

Warburton

231

Warburton Ra.

705 *Permits only*

Mt. Squires

Sutherland Ra.

Gibn

Axe Hill

Townsend Ridge

Mt. Laurie

L. Wells

Manton Knob
505

Baker Lake

6

Ernest Giles Ra.

574

Mi Mi Rocks

Sykes Bluff
490

G r e a

L. Throssel
Cosmo

172

Aboriginal

Land •519
Mt. Shentin

Yamarna

579

Yeo L.

*Yeo Lake
Nature Reserve*

Saunders Pt.
•528

164

Neale Junction
Nature Reserve

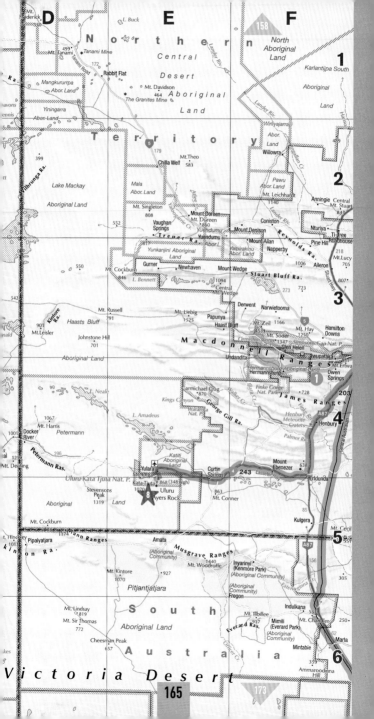

D   **E**   **F**

Mt. ederick
330
L. Buck

North Aboriginal Land
158

1

Mt. Tanami
499

Tanami Mine

N o r t h e r n

Central Desert

Lander Riv.

Karlantijpa South

Mangkururrpa
Abor. Land

Rabbit Flat

172

Aboriginal Land

Yiningarra
Abor. Land

Mt. Davidson
464
The Granites Mine

Mt. Davidson
A b o r i g i n a l Land

Wirliyajarra

Abor. Land

489

2

Ra.

399

Wilbunga Ra.

T e r r i t o r y

5
179

Chilla Well

Mt.Theo
583

Willowra

Pawu Abor. Land

Anningie Central
Mt. Stuart
843

Lake Mackay

Aboriginal Land

Mala Abor. Land

Mt. Singleton
808

Mala Abor. Land

Mt. Leichhardt
1140

Nturiya

Ti-Tree
Roadhouse

550

552

Vaughan Springs

Mt. Doreen
860

Mount Doreen

Yuendumu
Yuendumu Abor. L.

Mount Denison

Coniston

Pine Hill

Reynolds Ra.

218

Mt.Lucy
705

T r e u e r R a.

Yunkanjini Aboriginal Land

Yalpirakinu Abor. Land

Mount Allan

Napperby

1006

Aileron

807

3

Mt. Cockburn
846

Gurner

Newhaven

Mount Wedge

Stuart Bluff Ra.

L. Bennett

Mt 1094
Central
Mt Wedge

273

723

5424

Kintore Ra.

901
Mt.Leisler

Haasts Bluff
791

Mt. Russell

Mt. Liebig
1525

Papunya

Haast Bluff

Derwent

Narwietooma

Mt. Zeil 1166
1531
Mt. Sonder
1250
Ormiston Gorge

5
Mt. Hay

Hamilton Downs

Johnstone Hill
701

M a c d o n n e l l   R a n g e s

Mt. 1347
Ormiston Gorge
Glen Helen

Simpsons Gap Nat. P.

Twupataka

Aboriginal Land

Undandita

Hermannsburg Aboriginal Land
Hermannsburg

1
Owen Springs

203

Mt. Harris
1067

L. Neale

Docker River

Petermann

Carmichael Crag
870

Kings Canyon

Waratta Nat. P.

George Gill Ra.

James Ranges

Henbury Meteorite Craters

A87

728

4

1001

Petermann Ras.

296

121
Mt. Deering

Katiti Aboriginal Land

L. Amadeus

Finke Gorge Nat. P.

Palmer Riv.

A87
Henbury

Mount Ebenezer
638

Central Australia

Erldunda

Yulara
Mt 1066

Uluru-Kata Tjuta Nat. P.

Kata-Tjuta 868 (348 high)
1070

Curtin Springs
4
243

Lasseter Hwy.

85

8
Uluru
Ayers Rock

Stevensons Peak
1319

Aboriginal Land

863
Mt. Conner

Kulgera

Mt. Cecil

5

t. Hindley
1013

Pipalyatjara

Mann Ranges
1174

Amata
(Aboriginal Community)

Musgrave Ranges

Inyarinyi
(Kenmore Park)

A87

156

kin t o n Ra.

Mt. Kintore
1070

927

Mt. Woodroffe
1440

(Aboriginal Community)

Fregon

305

Everadinna Hwy.

Pitjantjatjara

S o u t h

Mt. Lindsay
819
Mt. Sir Thomas
772

Aboriginal Land

Mt. Illbillee
917

Mimili
(Everard Park)
(Aboriginal Community)

Everard Ras.

Indulkana

Mt. Chandler

250

Cheesman Peak
657

A u s t r a l i a

Mintabie

359
62

Marla

6

V i c t o r i a   D e s e r t

165

Ammaroodinna Hill

173

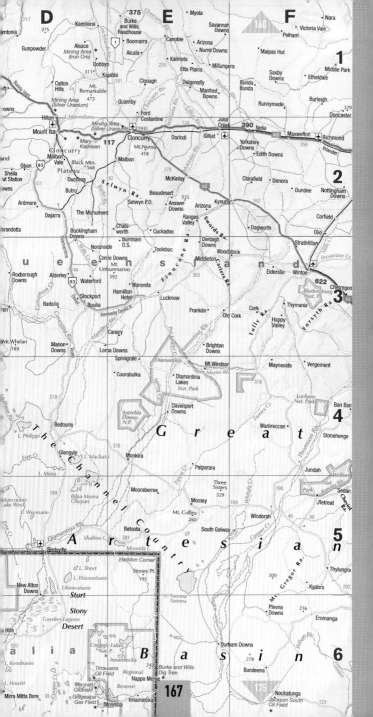

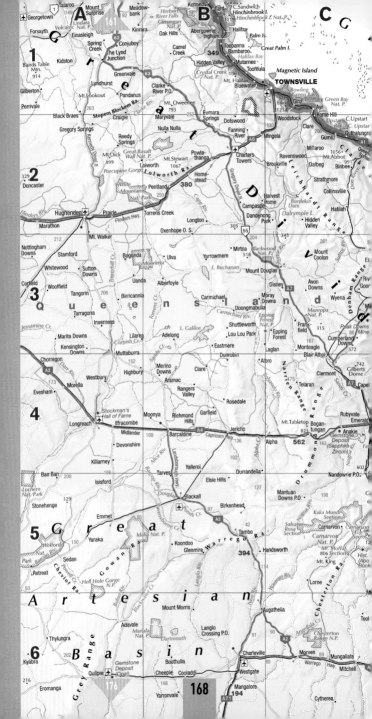

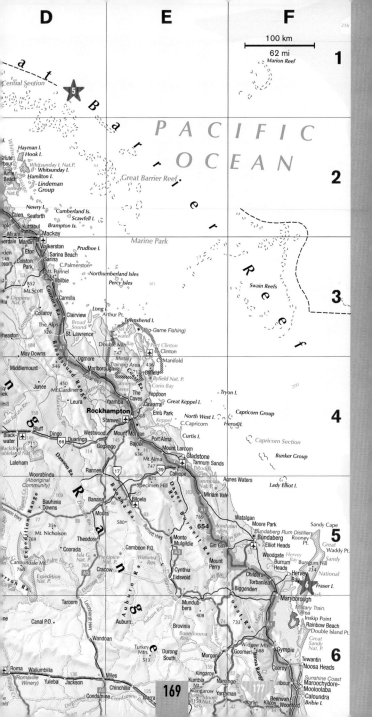

D

E

F

100 km
62 mi
Marion Reef

1

Central Section
★5

P A C I F I C

O C E A N

Hayman I.
Hook I.
Whitsunday I. Nat.P.
Whitsunday I.
Airlie Hamilton I.
Beach
Lindeman
Group
Nat.P.
Newry I.
Calen Seaforth
Kuttabul
Mirani Marian
Mackay

Great Barrier Reef

2

Walkerston
erdale Eton
Sarina
149 Colston Sarina Beach
Park Mt.Funnel
Cumberland Is.
Scawfell I.
Brampton Is.

Marine Park

Mt.Scott
Dippera
Nat.P.
Carmila

Northumberland Isles
Percy Isles

3

Collaroy
The Alps
526
St. Lawrence
May Downs
Clairview
Long Long
Arthur Pt.
Townshend I.
(Big-Game Fishing)

Swain Reefs

Middlemount
Ogmore
Marlborough
Byfield
Corio Bay

Double Mt.
Port Clinton
C.Clinton
Military
Training Area
436
C.Manifold
Byfield Nat. P.

Mt.Gardiner
546
Leura
Yaamba
The Caves
Cawarral
Yeppoon
Tryon I.

4

Rockhampton
Stanwell
Emu Park
Great Keppel I.
North West I.
C.Capricorn
Heron I.
Capricorn Group

Capricorn Section

Blackwater
Dingo
Duaringa
Westwood
Mount Morgan
608
Port Alma
Curtis I.

Bunker Group

Bluff
711
Gogango
Bajool
Mt.Alma
Mount Larcom

Laleham
Rannes
747
Gladstone
Tannum Sands

Agnes Waters
Lady Elliot I.

Wooralooba
(Aboriginal
Community)
Banana
Specimen Hill
Bilela
Calliope
Miriam Vale

5

Bauhinia
Downs
Moura
769
654
Watalgan
Moore Park
Bundaberg Rum Distillery
Bundaberg
Elliot Heads
Sandy Cape

Mt. Nicholson
769
Theodore
Cracow
Monto
Mulgildie
Gin Gin
Woodgate Hervey
Burrum
Heads
Burrum Hill
234
Great
Waddy Pt.
Sandy
National

Coorada
Camboon P.O.
Cynthia
Eidsvold
Mount
Perry
Childers
Torbanlea
Hervey
Bay
Fraser I.

6

Taroom
Mundubera
Biggenden
Maryborough
Military Train.
Area
Inskip Point
Rainbow Beach
Double Island Pt.

Canal P.O.
Auburn
Brovinia
Boondooma
Res.
733

Wandoan
Turkey
Mtn.
513
Durong
South
Murgon
Widgee Mtn.
Goomeri
688
Jimna Range
Gympie
Tewantin
Noosa Heads

Roma Wailumbilla
(Romavilla
Winery)
Yuleba Jackson
Miles
Chinchilla
Condamine
Warra
Kingaroy
Kumbia
Nanango
Yarraman
Jinna
Cooroy
Sunshine Coast
Maroochydore-
Mooloolaba
Caloundra
Bribie I.
Beerwah

169

177

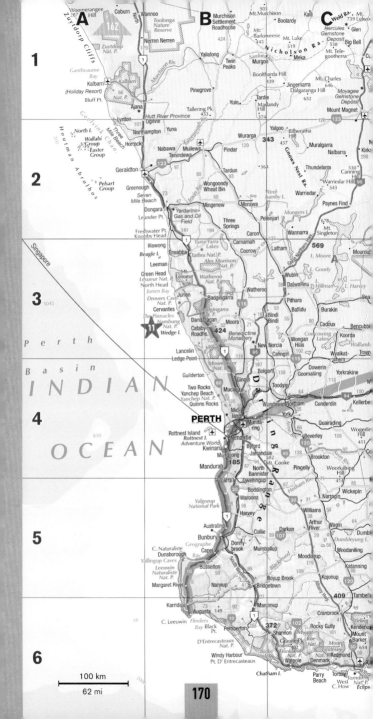

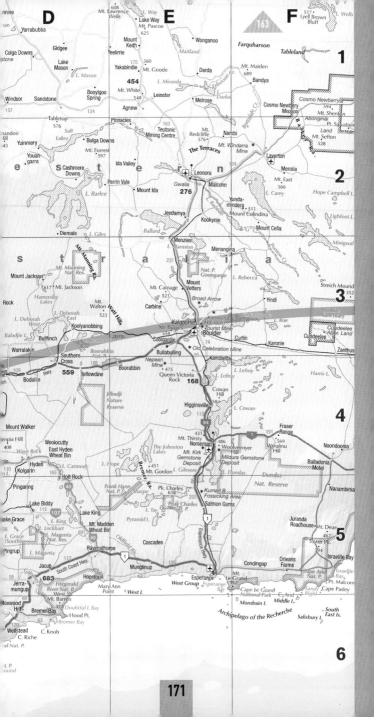

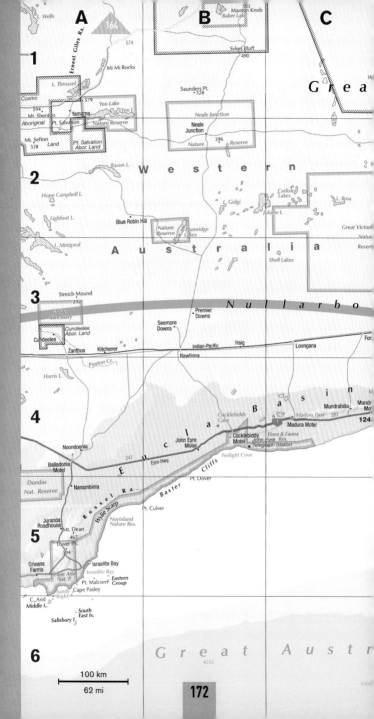

D · E · F

Mt. Lindsay
819
Mt. Sir Thomas
772
Cheesman Peak
657

Fregon
(Aboriginal
Community)
Indulkana
53
Mt. Chandler
250

1

Everard Ras.
165

Mintabie
Marla
936

Pitjantjatjara

Aboriginal   Land

Ammaroodinna
Hill
359

Oliver Cr.

V i c t o r i a   D e s e r t

Unnamed
Conservation Park

L. Meramangye

Tallaringa

Conservation

Park

2

rest
Lakes

S o u t h

Wyola Lake

Observatory Hill

L. Dey-Dey

Maralinga-Tjarutja

L. Maurice

Aboriginal Lands

A u s t r a l i a

Garford
Indooroopilly
Outstation
230

Wilkinson
Lakes

Half
Moon L.

Woomera

Prohibited

3

Military
Training
Area
(Entry Prohibited)

Maralinga

Yarle L.

Ooldea Ra.

Watson

Bates

Durkin
Outstation

Wynbring

P l a i n

Cook

Trans-Australian   Railway

Deakin

Fisher

Gould L.

Yellabinna

Nullarbor
Regional Reserve

Koonalda Cave
(Entry prohibited)

Ruins

Regional Reserve

n Buff
-graph
Station

Nullarbor Nat.-P.

A1

**Nullarbor
Roadhouse**

Yalata
523

Yalata

4

Eucla Motels

Head of
Bight

Aboriginal

Yumbarra Cons.

OTG International
Satellite Earth Station

me   +9h30 Gr. Time

Nundroo

Land

Coorabie
C. Adieu

Fowlers Bay

Penong

Ceduna

Maltee

Nuyts Reefs

Fowlers Bay

St. Peter I.

Denial
Bay

Smoky
Bay

Nuyts Archipelago

Pt. Brown
St. Francis
Isles

Smoky Bay

Streaky
Bay

Streaky Bay

5

65

Investigator
Group

6

l i a n   B i g h t

1390

2000

4000

200

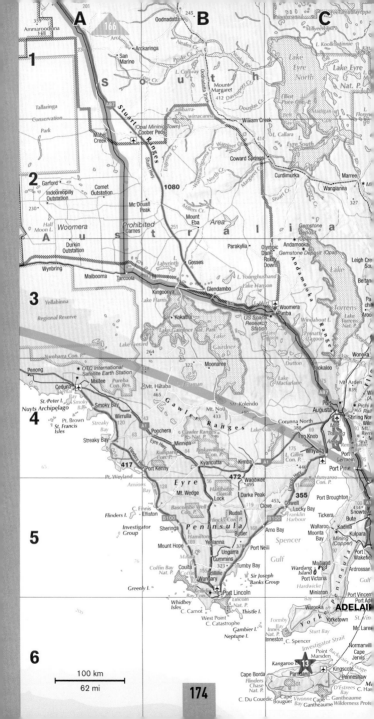

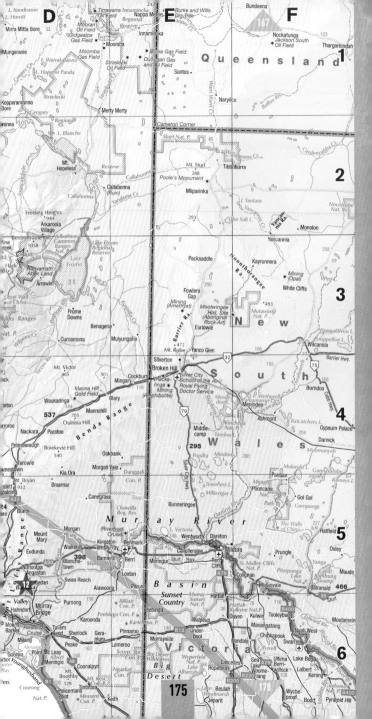

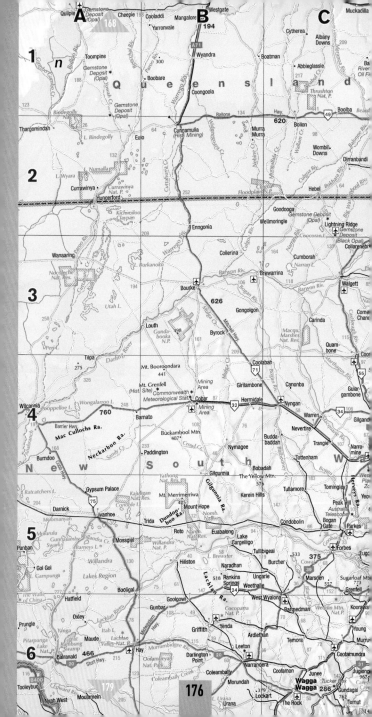

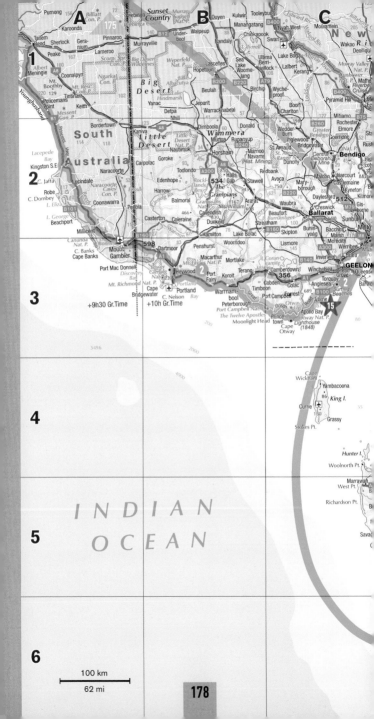

KEY TO ROAD ATLAS

Highway, multilane divided road - under construction Autobahn, mehrspurige Straße - in Bau	═══ ═ ═ ═ ═	Autoroute, route à plusieurs voies - en construction Autosnelweg, weg met meer rijstroken - in aanleg
Trunk road - under construction Fernverkehrsstraße - in Bau	——— — — — —	Route à grande circulation - en construction Weg voor interlokaal verkeer - in aanleg
Principal highway Hauptstraße		Route principale Hoofdweg
Secondary road Nebenstraße		Route secondaire Overige verharde wegen
Practicable road, track Fahrweg, Piste		Chemin carrossable, piste Weg, piste
Road numbering Straßennummerierung	E20 11 70 26 5 40 9	Numérotage des routes Wegnummering
Distances in kilometers Entfernungen in Kilometer	**259** 130 ↓ 129	Distances en kilomètres Afstand in kilometers
Height in meters - Pass Höhe in Meter - Pass	1365 •	Altitude en mètres - Col Hoogte in meters - Pas
Railway - Railway ferry Eisenbahn - Eisenbahnfähre	———	Chemin de fer - Ferry-boat Spoorweg - Spoorpont
Car ferry - Shipping route Autofähre - Schifffahrtslinie		Bac autos - Ligne maritime Autoveer - Scheepvaartlijn
Major international airport - Airport Wichtiger internationaler Flughafen - Flughafen	✈ ✈	Aéroport importante international - Aéroport Belangrijke internationale luchthaven - Luchthaven
International boundary - Province boundary Internationale Grenze - Provinzgrenze	▨▨▨▨▨▨	Frontière internationale - Limite de Province Internationale grens - Provinciale grens
Undefined boundary Unbestimmte Grenze	▨▨ ▨▨ ▨▨	Frontière d'Etat non définie Rijksgrens onbepaalt
Time zone boundary Zeitzonengrenze	-4h Greenwich Time • • • • • • • • -3h Greenwich Time	Limite de fuseau horaire Tijdzone-grens
National capital Hauptstadt eines souveränen Staates	**CANBERRA**	Capitale nationale Hoofdstad van een souvereine staat
Federal capital Hauptstadt eines Bundesstaates	<u>**Perth**</u>	Capitale d'un état fédéral Hoofdstad van een deelstat
Restricted area Sperrgebiet		Zone interdite Verboden gebied
National park Nationalpark		Parc national Nationaal park
Ancient monument Antikes Baudenkmal	∴	Monument antiques Antiek monument
Interesting cultural monument Sehenswertes Kulturdenkmal	✳ *Angkor Wat*	Monument culturel interéssant Bezienswaardig cultuurmonument
Interesting natural monument Sehenswertes Naturdenkmal	✳ *Ha Long Bay*	Monument naturel interéssant Bezienswaardig natuurmonument
Well Brunnen	⌣	Puits Bron
Trips & Tours Ausflüge & Touren		Excursions & tours Uitstapjes & tours
Perfect route Perfekte Route		Itinéraire idéal Perfecte route
MARCO POLO Highlight	★ 1	MARCO POLO Highlight

INDEX

This index lists all places and sights featured in this guide (NP = National Park). Numbers in bold indicate a main entry.

WRITE TO US

e-mail: info@marcopologuides.co.uk

Did you have a great holiday?
Is there something on your mind?
Whatever it is, let us know!
Whether you want to praise, alert us
to errors or give us a personal tip –
MARCO POLO would be pleased to
hear from you.
We do everything we can to provide the
very latest information for your trip.

Nevertheless, despite all of our authors'
thorough research, errors can creep in.
MARCO POLO does not accept any
liability for this. Please contact us by
e-mail or post.

MARCO POLO Travel Publishing Ltd
Pinewood, Chineham Business Park
Crockford Lane, Chineham
Basingstoke, Hampshire RG24 8AL
United Kingdom

PICTURE CREDITS
Cover photograph: kangaroo (Getty Images/Photodisc: Brakefield); Outback Uluru (mauritius images: Jostmeier)
DuMont Bildarchiv: Emmler (front flap left, 52/53, 92, 102/103, 104, 149); Leue (2 centre bottom, 15, 44/45, 79, 83), Widmann (66, 124, 135); B. Gebauer und S. Huy (1 bottom); Getty Images/Photodisc: Brakefield (1 top); David Haines, Joyce Hinterding and BREENSPACE (17 bottom); Huber: Huber (2 centre top, 32/33), Rellini (7, 76), Giovanni Simeone (109); M. Kirchgessner (125); R. Irek (129); Laif: Barbagallo (3 bottom, 9, 96/97), Emmler (3 centre, 28, 37, 75, 84/85, 106, 146 bottom), Heeb (24/25, 50, 58), hemis.fr (5, 6, 30 bottom, 34, 35, 86, 117, 127), La Roque (10/11, 48, 72, 133, 181), Lengler (81), Valentin (2 bottom, 30 top, 56/57); Laif/Arcaid: Gollings (60); Laif/hemis.fr: Dozier (119), Giuglio (63), Herve Hughes (39); H. Leue (3 top, 29, 68/69, 70, 78, 120/121, 136/137, 138/139, 142/143, 158/159); Livebait (17 top); Look: age fotostock (47), Dressler (46), Heeb (43), Wothe (110/111); mauritius images: age (18/19, 36, 98, 141), Alamy (26 right, 140, 142, 143), Boelter (122), Bridge (40/41), DK Images (2 top, 4), Fritz (147), Flirt (12/13), Jostmeier (1 top) Keyphotos (55); Torino (23); mauritius images/age: Grandadam (95), Kadic (8); mauritius images/imagebroker: Mayall (21); mauritius images/imagebroker/White Star: Gumm (64/65, 134); H. P. Merten (88); Okapia/BIOS: Watts (20); Riley Classic Balsawood Surfboards (16 centre); Ruby Rabbit: Josh Klapp (16 top); O. Stadler (front flap right); K. Thiele (116); T. P. Widmann (27, 28/29, 67, 90, 101, 112, 115, 130/131, 140/141); E. Wrba (22, 26 left, 132, 146 top); www.discology.com.au: Richard Sampson (16 bottom)

1st Edition 2013
Worldwide Distribution: Marco Polo Travel Publishing Ltd, Pinewood, Chineham Business Park,
Crockford Lane, Basingstoke, Hampshire RG24 8AL, United Kingdom. Email: sales@marcopolouk.com
© MAIRDUMONT GmbH & Co. KG, Ostfildern
Chief editor: Marion Zorn
Authors: Esther Blank, Urs Wälterlin; co-authors: Bruni Gebauer and Stefan Huy; editor: Manfred Pötzscher
Programme supervision: Anita Dahlinger, Ann-Katrin Kutzner, Nikolai Michaelis
Picture editors: Barbara Mehrl
What's hot: wunder media, Munich
Cartography road atlas & pull-out map: © MAIRDUMONT, Ostfildern
Design: milchhof : atelier, Berlin; Front cover, pull-out map cover, page 1: factor product munich
Translated from German by Christopher Wynne; editor of the English edition: Christopher Wynne
Prepress: M. Feuerstein, Wigel

DON'T ACT THE KNOW-ALL

Putting yourself first and bragging is something that won't go down well in Australia. That doesn't mean that you shouldn't make your own position clear when discussing something with an Australian. In fact, quite the opposite: they like people with a strong opinion about politics, for example, as long as it's not put across as if you were a know-all.

DON'T STAY LONGER THAN YOUR VISA ALLOWS

Australia has very strict immigration laws. Anyone whose visa runs out or works illegally will not just be extradited but will not be allowed to return for several years.

DON'T UNDERESTIMATE JELLYFISH

Stinger, box jellyfish or *sea wasp* are the names of murderously dangerous types of jellyfish – in fact just touching one can be deadly. A first-aid tip is to apply vinegar on the relevant patch of skin. Fortunately, these nasty creatures are only found in tropical coastal waters – and only between October and May. During this period you should only ever go into the sea in a wetsuit or go to beaches that are protected by nets. Further out to sea, for example around the islands on the Great Barrier Reef, there are – in most cases – no jellyfish.

DON'T BRING AN APPLE WITH YOU

Thanks to Australia's isolation, it has been spared various agricultural diseases – such as foot and mouth. To make sure it stays this way, a whole army of officers is waiting to meet people at your point of entry in Australia. Even as you come in to land at Sydney, you are warned not to take any foodstuffs with you. Fruit and meat are completely taboo, other articles (such as chocolate) are tolerated as long as you declare them on the customs form. If you break the law and the specially trained sniffer dogs or x-ray machines catch you, you will have to pay a heavy fine.

DON'T LOOK ABORIGINES IN THE EYE

Most Aborigines find it very unpleasant when someone looks straight at them when talking. This is just one of several social rules that you should observe when with Aborigines. Another is not to talk about unpleasant or embarrassing subjects such as poverty, hygiene or sex. But there are also certain rules of etiquette which equally well apply to white Australians. For example, it is often considered inappropriate in many places for a man to shake hands with a woman as a form of welcome.